"Finally, your YouTube videos don't have to look like they were shot with your parents' video camera even if they were shot with your parents' video camera."

— Mike Rotman, CEO/founder, *Streamin' Garage.com*

"The title of Jay Miles' new book *Conquering YouTube* does not do its content justice. Any filmmaker, whether making Web videos or features, will benefit from Jay's clearly written treatise, which cleverly disguises advanced techniques in the common language of every Everyman with a digital video camera."

— Bobby Bognar, host, History Channel's *Food Tech*

"There is something here for everyone, no matter if you are a skilled professional or a novice videographer. Miles has created "The Bible" for social media production! It is in an easy-to-follow format, allowing quick reference for problem-solving, with clear and helpful illustrative photos. A must for anyone trying to take his or her video project to the next level!"

— Ted Yasi, cameraman, ABC World News

"Jay Miles has written a how-to manual that's perfect for at-home TV producers and filmmakers. He has broken through the mystery and magic of the process to show you that it really can be easy."

— Mark Bellotti, senior producer, *NHL on Versus*

"Don't be fooled by the title of Jay Miles' book, *Conquering YouTube*. This is a serious treasure of knowledge for everyone who wants to tell stories with images and sounds. The book's metaphor of "tips" belies the wisdom contained in the text and instructive photographs. One example out of 100: Even the pros forget the wisdom of shooting the "E and Es." Miles not only defines the problem but also offers ways to solve problems to create more effective stories. And best of all, Miles delivers this wealth of instruction in a highly readable, personable style."

— Peter Moller, professor, S. I. Newhouse School of Public Communications, Syracuse University

"This is a terrific resource for young filmmakers who want to make more professional-looking and creative videos. Written in a breezy, witty, and engaging style, this highly readable book is full of tips, tricks, and advice that will help novice directors make videos that will stand out from the pack."

— Michael D. Calia, director, Ed McMahon Communications Center, and associate professor, communications (adjunct), School of Communications, Quinnipiac University

"Accomplished videographer, producer, and teacher, Jay Miles helps the novice and experienced shooter shoot better. Whether you're a new or experienced camera operator, Jay Miles' *Conquering YouTube* will improve your skills and productions. Everything you need to make videos and make 'em better. Jay Miles' decades of working as a professional videographer, producer, and teacher are expertly summarized in this easy-to-read book. You will make better videos. Highly recommended!"

— Don Schwartz, *CineSource* Magazine
http://DonSchwartz.com
http://CineSourceMagazine.com/index.php?/site/DSchwartz

"Jay Miles' experience and wit make this easy-to-follow video-course-in-a-book a valuable tool for aspiring creators. Practice his tips and hints and your videos will stand out in a big (and hopefully profitable) way!"

— Ken Simon, executive producer, SimonPure Productions

"I love *Conquering YouTube*. It packs in a lot of very valuable information for budding filmmakers. Would love to use it with schools!"

— Dominique Lasseur, executive director, Global Village Media; independent filmmaker

"Forget YouTube... this book is a grade-A primer for anyone learning to shoot video, whether it's for the Internet or Sundance. Using straightforward, easy-to-read explanations and helpful photos, Jay Miles has created an indispensable handbook for any young filmmaker."

— Chad Gervich, writer, producer, *Wipeout*, *Reality Binge*, *Speeders*, *Foody Call*; author: *Small Screen, Big Picture: A Writer's Guide to the TV Business,* http://cgervich@avantguild.com

"As a former student and current working colleague of Jay's, I can only say this book is pure magic. The way he attacks the fundamental and more advanced creative skills makes them extremely easy to understand, and more importantly, really makes them stick long after you've done the lessons. So for anyone looking to get into filming or expand your creative palette — this book is a must!"

— David Brown, founder, DB Studios Multimedia

Jay Miles Conquering YouTube:

101 Pro Video Tips to Take You to the Top

Published by Michael Wiese Productions
12400 Ventura Blvd. #1111
Studio City, CA 91604
tel. 818.379.8799
fax 818.986.3408
mw@mwp.com
www.mwp.com

Cover Design: Johnny Ink *www.johnnyink.com*
Cover Photograph: Norwin Hatschbach
Book Design: Gina Mansfield Design
Editor: Pamela Grieman

Printed by McNaughton & Gunn, Inc., Saline, Michigan
Manufactured in the United States of America
Printed on Recycled Stock

Library of Congress Cataloging-in-Publication Data

Miles, Jay, 1969-
  Conquering YouTube : 101 pro tips to take you to the top / Jay
Miles.
     p. cm.
  ISBN 978-1-932907-94-0
1. YouTube (Electronic resource) 2. Internet videos--Production
and direction. 3. Video recordings--Production and direction. 4.
Digital video--Production and direction. 5. Webcasting. I. Title.
  TK5105.8868.Y68M44 2011
  006.6'96--dc22
                                        2011002602

Mixed Sources
Product group from well-managed
forests and other controlled sources
www.fsc.org Cert no. SW-COC-002283
© 1996 Forest Stewardship Council
FSC

CONTENTS

ACKNOWLEDGMENTS

It's simply impossible for me to thank everyone who in some way, large or small, known or unknown, helped to make this book possible. For the messages and phone calls, questions and suggestions, reality checks and encouragements, I am most grateful to an enormous pool of family, friends, teachers, students, colleagues, fellow dreamers, divine fools, and cosmic clowns. Bits and pieces of you all are with me in many ways, every day.

I am thankful for the support, trust, and guidance that I received from Michael Wiese, Ken Lee, Mark Travis, and many others affiliated with MWP. Thank you to my fellow writers for your positive energy. Thank you, producers and employers, for keeping me working, thinking, seeing, and striving. Thank you to my fellow crew members for trusting me to lead, insisting that I follow, and allowing me to grow along the way.

To my many inspiring teachers and students, both traditional and unexpected, may I continue to learn twice as much from you as I might hope to teach. To my closest friends, near and far, who believed in me, tolerated me, motivated, challenged, and enlightened me, my journey continues to be meaningful, soulful, joyous, and thrilling, thanks to all of you.

Lastly, a huge thank you to both of my parents for taking me to the library *and* to the movies, for letting me watch TV, and for making me turn it off to go outside and play.

HOW TO USE THIS BOOK

There is an insane amount of video on YouTube, full of memorable moments, hilarious comedy, riveting drama, and informative content. The only problem is that tons of that video is poorly lit, suffers from bad audio, gets compromised by shaky camera work, becomes soured by strange colors, and is generally afflicted by elements that scream "Amateur!"

This book is designed to give you all the tools you need to avoid these pitfalls, while helping you to make exciting, engaging, and effective videos for the Web. These tips can help you reach another level with projects that you can create, manipulate, edit, and record in a manner that is consistent with professional video productions. I have gathered these tips from hundreds of hours on TV and movie sets; from music video, advertising, and corporate shoots; and from hours of trying — and struggling — with my own efforts. And I have streamlined each process so that these skills can be mastered by you in a manageable, memorable, and productive way.

You can work through the tips from start to finish, gradually improving your skills, or you can pick an interesting section and master just those techniques. You can complete each exercise in order, building on skills from previous sections, or dip into a particular area so that your current project can truly benefit. Either way, this book walks you through industry-proven insider tricks that professionals use every day to improve shots, scenes, and setups. The majority of the exercises have been tested (and proven effective) in high school and college video classes I've taught and on paid gigs that I have completed all across the country. So I know that they work, I want them to work for you, and I want you not only to improve your images, shots, and edits, but gain confidence and have fun as you progress.

The book is grouped into eight major sections: collections of tips and exercises that flow together. The first section, "Rules of the Road," gives you a number of important tips for getting started in an organized, professional manner, helping you to manage both your equipment and your approach to shooting quality video. Next, the "Basics" section walks you through traditional shots, framings, camera moves, and applications and helps you deal with common problems as you begin to shoot. The section called "Light and Shadows" will help you conquer lighting problems and help you discover interesting lighting solutions, using both proven and innovative (also known as "affordable!") techniques. The "Special Effects" section outlines simple and manageable ways to wow your viewers with a variety of awesome in-camera and postproduction tricks. The "Intermediate" section pushes you a little further, helping you master additional camera techniques, deal with actor movement and placement, explore more visually arresting compositions and framings, and explore more elaborate approaches to shooting and editing. The "Advanced" section addresses more complex cinematic applications, trickier camera functions and methodologies, more elaborate video setups, and tips for moving camera operations. And finally, the "Editing" and "Audio" sections will help you solve common problems with sound, postproduction audio work, graphics, and microphone and boom issues. You'll also explore professionally proven steps for capturing great sound and for editing video effectively.

It is equally important to consider *why* you will want to master the tips explained in this book. For many, simply improving the look, sound, and transitions included in your videos will be motivation enough. For others, addressing specific areas of concern or particular problems that plague your videos will give you a reason to try a new approach, explore an alternative answer, or strengthen a certain set of skills. For beginners, working through each tip and each exercise will allow you to progress rapidly and to avoid the most troubling mistakes made by amateur videographers. For more advanced shooters, you will be able to target a specific challenge (dealing with green screens, for example), finding workable solutions in just that tip or section.

The applications for the tips outlined in this book are almost limitless. You may find a creative way to complete an otherwise dull assignment for school or for your employer. You might discover a novel approach for presenting your resume, portfolio, promotion, special event, or advertisement. You can jazz up an otherwise traditional application to college or generate a change in your career. You may uncover a more immediate, engaging way to address students, employees, clients, partners, or customers. You can improve the quality of highlight videos for sports teams, family events, concerts, and vacations. You can help break the next big indie rock band or hip-hop star by shooting their first music video — or grab the attention of Hollywood honchos, journalists, TV producers, politicians or (hopefully!) investors by uploading a video blog, news show, talk show, or documentary.

You can use the tips in this book to create videos that change opinions, careers, minds, and attitudes. You can improve your grades, performance, profits, and position. Your videos can reach countless viewers, win contests, promote healthy and positive causes, and deliver timely and effective messages — all while you enjoy fun, fantastic adventures that result in digital fireworks that will help you to conquer YouTube. In other words, you can change your world, your outlook, and your life. All you need to do now is take a breath, pick a tip, and start shooting.

INTRODUCTION

This book assumes several things about who you are and what you are doing right now. It assumes that you own (or are about to buy) a video camera (Figure 1.1), that you love to shoot, that every ounce of your soul is screaming to make better videos, and that you don't mind waiting ages for the light to be right, for transitions to render, or for an actor to become available. It also assumes that you can muster up a good attitude, a willingness to improve, and the courage to face your fears, challenge your eye, and embrace your inner Hitchcock.

Figure 1.1

This book assumes that you can also endure errors and that you can, in turn, learn from those errors. I'll tell you a little video secret: I have a shoebox filled with awful, terrible, can't-show-it-to-anybody footage — wobbly pans, shots all out of focus, tacky zooms — tons of beginner video that represents hours of trying, failing, learning, and trying again, only better. This book assumes that you are ready to follow a similar path: to shoot, review your footage, and then reshoot to improve your efforts, your skills, and, ultimately, your videos. It assumes that you are open to new ideas, able to acknowledge mistakes, and ready to capture the world — one frame, shot, or camera move at a time.

These are time-tested, surefire methods from the creative side of the camera, the side where you start taking command of your own visual storytelling. It won't matter what brand of camera you have, if you shoot to tape or hard disc, or edit on a PC or a Mac. By absorbing these camera, lighting, editing, and special effects tips, your videos will be primed to take off. As they do, be sure to stop by www.jmilestv.com. That's where you can find additional help, tips, clips, information, and more. We're all on an amazing journey, shooting as we go, and I look forward to helping you to take the first step.

Ready? Good. Let's get to work.

SECTION 1
RULES OF THE ROAD ▶

TIP 1
AUTOMATION NATION

We live in an amazing time. The machines that fill our lives complete more and more tasks for us: cars that find their way home, phones that download music while we sleep, websites that negotiate bargain flights. But all of this automation is actually compromising our ability to make good video. When you allow your camera to set your focus, white balance, and framing, you end up with a compromised image that doesn't truly reflect what you see in your mind's eye, and that doesn't enable you to fully explore your potential as a visual storyteller. In other words, you are relying on your camera to guess how the various aspects of your images are captured. And this can create huge problems.

The solution? You must become a master of all of the manual settings that your camera allows. You need to break free from the deception that "automatic" equals "better." In this first section of tips, you will explore the key camera settings that all professional videographers control for every single shot they complete. At first, these tasks may seem dreary, cumbersome, or awkward. At first, you'll forget more than you can remember. But with a little patience, a little practice, and a willingness to put in the time, you will absorb these duties and master their possibilities.

The best shooters that I have worked with complete these tasks almost instinctively, their fingers finding the knobs and controls effortlessly, their eye catching slight variances in each image as they make adjustments. I encourage you to set this as your goal. By mastering the manual functions on your camera, you will not only make better videos, but will free yourself from the constraints of the automatic and reach a new level of visual storytelling that will set your work apart from the rest of the pack.

TIP 2
THREE LEGS TO STAND ON

One of the biggest mistakes made by aspiring directors is relying on handheld shots. Your new camera comes out of the box, slips onto your palm, and you are off and running, full of excitement and ideas, and… the only problem? Your shots are inconsistent, shaky, and difficult for the rest of us to watch.

This is a phenomenon I call the "Blair Witch Syndrome," and it strikes down countless new filmmakers. This affliction convinces newbie shooters that *all* their shots can be handheld, regardless of the story. To be fair, *The Blair Witch Project* was exciting and memorable, and effectively employed handheld shots perhaps more than any other flick. But you aren't shooting that movie. No matter how steady you think you are, all of us shake, stumble, and wiggle enough that hand-held shots quickly become unwatchable, amateur-looking jumbles. The answer? Buy a good tripod and master every aspect of this device: pans, tilts, loose settings, and tighter settings (Figure 2.1).

You must consider your tripod as an extension of the camera. More than a fancy lens, filter, or memory stick, the tripod is the most underappreciated tool you own. It gets left in car trunks, closets, lockers, or your uncle's house after the fourth of July. Don't make this mistake. Filmmakers have been schlepping their tripods, or "sticks," up mountains and stairways, down rivers and hallways, and across ice sheets and parking lots for more than a century. The reason? They realized that a pan should always look like a pan. Not a "sorta-kinda pan" with lots of jerky up-and-down gyrations. The Emmy–award-winning shooters that I know all follow one rule: Where the camera goes, the sticks go, too. Make sure that you embrace this practice.

Figure 2.1

TOP TIPS FOR STICKS

1. Keep It Tight: Lock your tripod off whenever you step away, including the telescoping legs. The more expensive the camera, the more likely it is to topple over when you turn away. Also, when panning, lock off your tilt, and vice versa.

2. Spread 'Em: Speaking of falling cameras, always make sure that the three legs are all spread out the maximum distance from the center. Anything else will lead to uneven shots, frustration, wasted time, or worse (camera + concrete + falling = bad).

3. It's a Drag: Decent tripods feature an adjustable range of resistance, from super tight to super loose, called drag. Play with it. Embrace it. Learn to love it. Once you find your "sweet spot," drag gives you smoother, even camera moves. Remember — a little resistance from the tripod is a *good* thing.

4. Bubble Boy: Most tripods come with a small leveling bubble, like the carpenter's tool. This helps you set a level horizon line, even on a rough surface. A friend of mine loves bubbles so much that he superglues them to cheaper tripods. I tend to use the bottom edge of the viewfinder to level my horizon. Either way, make sure you're straight — otherwise your subjects will look like they are climbing uphill.

5. Stiff Arm: The better tripods give you an adjustable control arm. This should point toward you (opposite your lens). The rest is up to you — spin it, point it up, down, sideways, whatever feels best. Then lock it off. Also, make sure the plate that attaches to the camera is pointing the right way. Yes, you can shoot with the camera pointing sideways (and you can stumble on some cool Dutch angles this way), but it limits your ability to tilt properly. Proceed with caution.

TIP 3
SHOOT FIRST, ASK QUESTIONS LATER

Training the eye is a process that can take years. One of the tricks that I have discovered to train my eye and keep my skills sharp is to shoot first and ask questions later. In other words, it's almost time to put this book down and start shooting. Almost.

But before you rush off, camera in hand, to take your first steps into moviemaking, be sure to make yourself a promise. You must be willing to shoot and shoot and shoot. But, perhaps more importantly, you then need to sit down, concentrate, and review each shot, each camera move, and each lighting situation. Ask yourself as many critical questions as you can. Is my horizon line level? Is my tilting even, or jerky? Do I need to slow down my handheld camera moves (probably!)? Keep a journal. Log each attempted shot into a notebook, and write down what went wrong and what you can do better next time.

Write down the various camera settings as you shoot. Try the same shot several times, adjusting a particular function or setting (iris, shutter, white balance, etc.) one degree at a time. Watching the footage later, with these notes in hand, should help you quickly see what each setting (or each degree of a setting) on your camera can achieve. You will start to spot your own limitations, as well as your inherent strengths.

Shoot the exact same shot, a wide shot of your street, for example, at different times of the day or the year. How does different light affect your image? What camera functions can compensate for the lighting? Above all, make mistakes. Then go make some more mistakes. Then watch the footage, painful as it may be, and find out which errors need to be addressed and which skills you have mastered. Remember my secret shoebox of horrible footage? It's time to start filling yours.

THE GREAT MISTAKES

As with all of the exercises in this book, stay off private property, obey any (relevant!) laws, and know that video cameras often make people nervous. STOP if they get edgy, curious, combative, or just creepy. Stop if they think *you* are getting creepy!

1. **The street where you live:** Shoot a wide shot of your street at one-hour intervals. Note how the light changes. Explore which camera functions help you adjust to the changing light. For the more adventurous, repeat this shot for a week, a month, or a year.

2. **Sunrise/Sunset:** Repeat this same simple exercise, this time shooting out of the window of your living room. Mark the location for your tripod so you can recreate the exact shot over time. Shoot thirty seconds every hour. Or shoot thirty seconds once a week. Note how the lighting changes as the day, or the year, passes by your door.

3. **A day at the beach:** Head to the beach to practice panning. Using this long, (hopefully) unbroken horizon line, keep your pan moving at a steady rate for as long as possible. Then pan back the other way. Find a lighthouse (or telephone poles, light poles, umbrella stands, whatever) and practice tilting the same way, smoothly up and down. Repeat these moves at different speeds, keeping the shot steady and the speed consistent.

4. **In the ballpark:** Head to a ball field, town square, or skate park — any place that doesn't contain pro athletes or entail some sort of... um, trespassing. Find something (Frisbee, a ball game, people walking dogs) that involves *events being repeated*. Shoot the action using different framings, camera angles, or camera positions — but NO ZOOMS (I'll explain why later). Concentrate on keeping people and action in the shot, which should get more difficult with tighter framings. The challenges in each framing will reveal any inconsistencies or weaknesses when you review the footage later. Don't get frustrated! This is your first attempt — you will get better each time you shoot.

5. **Freestyle:** Go ahead — you've earned it. Carve out a two-hour block of time and go shoot anything and everything that catches your eye: textures, shapes, people, boats, trees, hot rods. Then spend an hour looking back at the shots. Are you zooming too much? Panning too fast? Don't worry — you'll get better. How will you know? Because you should *repeat* these same shots *after* finishing the tips in this book. Be sure to watch both sets of clips when you are done to see how you have progressed!

TIP 4
NOT EASY BEING GREEN

You did it — made the calls, did the schmoozing, and got backstage access with your camera to interview that super-hip indie band. You race home, ready to hit the video blogosphere, only to recoil in horror when you see that the new face of rock looks… green?

What happened? You didn't set the white balance correctly. Or you left the camera in auto and it guessed wrong! (I warned you!) Remember, the camera is an amazing tool, but it's only as smart as you *tell it* to be. Incorrect skin tones, colors, and backgrounds can be avoided by setting the white balance *every time* you shoot.

And the best part? It's easy. By setting the white balance, you tell the camera what "white" is, and therefore help it capture all the other colors correctly (white light contains all the visible colors). Bingo — skin tones, fabrics, hair color, sunsets — they all look great.

Here's how:

1. Turn off the auto settings!

2. Find the white balance control. This may be on a menu, a wheel, or a button on the camera body itself. It will almost always look like two triangles topped by a square or sometimes a circle. I call this the "Alien Crop Circle Icon" because that's what it reminds me of. Now, here's the crucial part.

3. Zoom *all the way* in to a white surface. This can be a piece of foam core, notebook paper, a T-shirt of a crew member, a blank billboard. It doesn't matter — as long as it is white.

4. Activate the white balance. This will mean pushing that button or activating that menu item. The "Crop Circle" icon will usually blink for a few seconds, or the square might change from "empty" to a filled-in version. Bam! There's a shift in color and you're white balanced!

5. Remember — the white card *must be in the light source* you are using. If you are shooting under a streetlight at night, the white card needs to be *in* that pool of light. You can't just hold it two inches from the lens and get an accurate setting. If you can't fill the frame with white, move the camera closer, but *don't* move the white out from the light!

TOP TIPS FOR
WHITE BALANCE

IF YOU DO *ANY* OF THE FOLLOWING, YOU MUST RESET THE WHITE BALANCE:

▶ Move locations from inside to outside, or vice versa

▶ Power the camera off and back on again

▶ Change batteries

▶ Change the light source significantly

▶ Even a change in camera angle or costumes can cause havoc!
Trust your eyes!

PINK'S REVENGE

In addition to noting how your image will change when you set the white balance correctly, spend a few minutes setting this function *incorrectly*. Yeah, you read right. Zoom in on a blue sign, a green panel, a pink sheet of paper, and then activate your white balance. Zoom back out to see how this negatively affects skin tones, fabrics, and lighting. It's a great way to train your eye; practice setting white balance and convincing yourself why it is so important to set correctly, each and every time.

The best shooters that I know snap off a white balance so fast, I often don't even notice. Like most of the skills in this book, the more you practice, the faster you become, and the more natural these chores will become. This should be your goal — running through white balance, focus, and iris quickly and naturally before each shot. How do I control focus and iris settings? Read on!

TIP 5
A SHARPER IMAGE

Wait! Don't move! While you are zoomed in on a white surface (in the light!), hang out a minute and set the next crucial function on your camera: focus. Why set the focus when you are zoomed in? Isn't it harder this way to tell what is *in* focus and what *isn't*? Maybe at first, but this technique helps you avoid another frustrating default function of most cameras.

Have you ever seen that random rectangle in the middle of your viewfinder? It's there because most manufacturers assume that you want the action in the center to be in focus. This may be okay, except that most memorable cinematic images are framed off-center (see Tip 21), or deal with subjects that are different distances from your lens. So you need to *ignore* the rectangle (hint: turn this display option *off* in your menu), and set the focus they way you want it to be.

You do this by setting the focus on an object *farthest* from your lens. While you are zoomed in, frame up on a small, detailed object (an eyelash, a fingernail, a necklace) and adjust the focus until this minute detail is super sharp. Zoom back out and the *entire image* should now be in focus. This is a surefire way to grab a bunch of sharp shots. It also means that you can move your camera around (to a certain degree) to follow the action. There are instances when you will want to set

a more precise focus at a different distance from your lens (Tip 72), but for now you should ignore the center of the frame, ignore the comfort of the auto focus setting, and keep everything nice and crisp.

The only time you *should* rely on auto focus is for action-heavy sequences: shooting on a moving skateboard, in a moving car, on an airplane, while skydiving, or while chasing your dogs (or actors, or ex-boyfriend) through a field. Obviously, if you change camera angles drastically — the position of your subject changes, you move to a new spot that alters the depth in the shot, or the distance between your lens and the subject changes (moving from a block away from your house to a shot of your house from the front lawn, for example) — you need to repeat this process. Sound easy? It is. Now go practice.

TIP 6
PASSING THE VOIGHT-KAMPFF TEST

Just as our eyes are able to adjust when we leave a bright interior to find our way across a dark exterior, the camera makes a similar, physical adjustment to allow more or less light into the lens. This is controlled by an element called the iris, a circular opening after the lens that can increase or decrease in size. This diameter is measured using F-stops, and entire books have been written about this function, but you only need to remember that the larger the iris opening, the more light that enters your camera (and vice versa). And this is usually a good thing: Video cameras feed off of light, smashing this physical information into their sensory chips, translating it into electronic information, which we see as digital images. The downside? Our old nemesis: automatic settings.

If I had a dollar for every time I have seen videos in which the camera automatically reacted to a change in light, I would have… well, a lot of dollars. This is usually bad because your image can be momentarily blown out (too much light) or too dim (not enough), and the in-between moments give your work a cheap, amateurish look. To be fair, if you are moving from inside to outside quickly, or panning significantly, the change in light can be difficult to manage, and keeping the camera on auto iris might seem like the best solution.

However, a better approach is to locate your iris function (this might be a menu item or a physical control), select manual, and start making adjustments. Using a light meter (a device that measures light intensity) can help here, if you know the corresponding F-stop. If not, it's time to practice. Spend an entire day shooting in as many different lighting conditions as possible. Make adjustments as often as needed, understanding that more light is usually better than not enough. This is why "night" scenes are bathed in blue light. The camera needs light to function and blue has become an accepted way to depict night scenes dramatically while still making sure enough light is hitting the sensors.

TOP TIPS FOR
IRIS CONTROL

AS YOU MAKE IRIS ADJUSTMENTS, KEEP THESE TIPS IN MIND:

▶ Don't be afraid to adjust past a good setting, one or two F-stops, over-exposing your image. Then you can iris back down to "lock in" the right setting before shooting.

▶ Overexposing can be an interesting artistic choice, especially for dream sequences, flashbacks, or historical re-creations. I wouldn't advise it, however, when shooting an interview with the mayor or a star athlete.

▶ When in doubt, add light. Use "clip" lights, flash lights, work lights, or a desk lamp (see Tips 27 and 32). You can use a blue gel to simulate night or darken the image slightly in editing. Just remember that it's much harder to *add light later* successfully.

▶ Watch your other settings, as a change in iris can affect focus, and vice versa.

▶ Avoid adding "gain," which increases the video signal *within* the camera, but doesn't actually increase the amount of light entering the lens. This can "brighten" your shot, but often results in a grainy or thin image. You might add gain in extremely dark situations, like nightclubs, but should only do so as a last resort.

▶ Don't depend on your viewfinder screen. These often have separate brightness controls and can present you with a false impression of the exposure. It's worth it to lug an external monitor to your shoot, one that you tested *before* leaving for the location. This can be a small TV or a portable video monitor (they've gotten cheaper and smaller). Play a DVD with which you are familiar and make sure that the color, tint, brightness, and sharpness settings on this monitor are correct. Then plug your camera in, white balance, and double check the image on your external monitor.

TIP 7

SHUTTER TO THINK

Videos are a complete illusion. They are actually thirty different images, called frames, presented every second, which taken together fool our eyes into thinking that we are seeing movement. Hence the term *motion pictures* (although with film this illusion occurs at 24 frames per second, or fps, and PAL cameras shoot at 25 fps).

Playing with this speed allows us to capture two effective techniques. By increasing the frame rate, we expose more images per second, thus increasing the amount of information contained in each second, giving us the illusion of slow-motion. Conversely, reducing the frame rate limits the information in each second, skipping pieces of the action and giving us fast-motion: sped-up, frantic movement often associated with comedy. Reduce this even more drastically and you end up with dramatic images generally known as time-lapse footage.

Be aware that there is also an adjustment called shutter speed, which is not the same thing as the frame rate. While your fps determines how many images will be recorded per second, the shutter speed dictates how long the shutter in your camera will stay open (in fractions of a second) as you allow light to enter, creating an image. In general, with video, changes in shutter speed are less distinct than they are with film, but be sure to take note of which controls your camera includes and how these affect the resulting image.

Cameras more commonly come with a varying range of control over frame rates. I would encourage you to play, shooting test footage of your friends in the backyard tossing a Frisbee around. See what result you can get with different frame rates. Can you capture slow- and fast-motion clips? I tend to shy away from changing this too much, both because the TV gigs that I book most often are shot at a normal rate (or something called "drop frame," which is shot at 29fps to adjust for the number of seconds in an actual day), but also because most editing software has gotten much, much better at allowing me to explore these two extreme effects in postproduction.

But go play! Try different settings, repeating the same action each time. You may find that you like the "look" of in-camera slow- and fast-motion more than the digitally determined version. Remember that adjustments to shutter speed or frame rate can drastically affect your focus, depth of field, and exposure settings. You may need to readjust your focus or iris, depending on how your camera functions, the light, and the action you are shooting.

TIP 8

PREPARATION IS YOUR SALVATION

When students and other upcoming videographers ask me for advice about buying mikes or additional lenses or special accessories, I always say the same thing: Buy more batteries! And you should do the same. Without knowing what you will be shooting most often (sports, films, family events), it's impossible to discuss the range of possible accessories you could add to your camera, except one: batteries.

Yes, they're expensive, with impossible-to-remember product numbers, and many are tough to track down, but it's all worth it. Why? Because there's nothing worse than being three shots away from finishing a huge day, at a location that took you six months to get approval to use, when the sun is setting and — bang! Your battery dies. Buy two or three backups. Charge them for *at least* twenty-four hours *before you first use them*. Slap some colored tape across the back of each one, or white tape with a numbering system so you can keep track of which one needs juice (Figure 8.1). And bring your AC charger/adaptor with you (Figure 8.2).

Most of these won't charge a "brick" at the same time as running your camera, so plan carefully. Regardless of your circumstances, keep your backups charging.

Speaking of backups, you can never have too much tape. Tape has gotten so cheap that you can't afford *not* to have extras with you. If you shoot to a card, hard drive, disc, or other internal media, buy an extra one or get your raw footage dumped to a hard drive as soon as you can. Cameras get dropped, damaged, stolen, and lost — don't let your footage suffer the same fate. Keep a copy of the *unedited* clips for future backup, reference, or use. Or, in the event of the unthinkable, to replace what was on the camera. At the end of the day, it isn't about the camera, the location, or the star actor: It's about the footage.

Figure 8.1

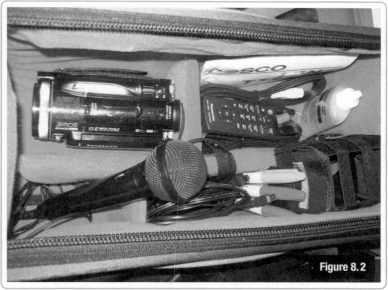

Figure 8.2

TIP 9
STAY ON TARGET!

What's the one shot they always include in those behind-the-scene segments on DVDs? The one where the crew member smacks the arm of the slate shut, the first assistant director calls "Rolling!" and the director yells "Action!"

Why? Because everyone who sees it thinks it's cool! This simple action screams "I'm making a legit movie!" Oh, and also because this is how big-time crews keep track of footage and sync it to sound in postproduction. Okay, since you don't have a big union crew and you're shooting in-camera audio, you don't need to slate your shots, right? Wrong.

Dropping a slate before every shot or every take of a complex scene can be the difference between sanity and digital madness. Maintain a running, written list

Figure 9.1

Figure 9.2

of which shots were "keepers" using the same numerical notation on your slate. If this feels like too much, simply shooting a "head slate" at the start of a short project will keep you from losing your mind, as well. All you need to include is the name of the project, the director's name, the date, and any other useful, short information (exterior vs. interior, day vs. night, type of audio). Don't forget to mark which channels the audio is on — your editor will thank you.

You can buy a wide range of dry-erase slates, from simple "clapboards" to more complex (and expensive) versions that digitally sync the time code from the audio deck. Or you can do what I do and buy a cheap dry-erase board at an office supply store (Figure 9.2). The important thing is to USE IT. Roll a minimum of thirty seconds for each head slate. Why? If you only use twenty minutes on a DV tape and then shoot an unrelated project with a thirty-second head slate, when you cue through the footage later, it's easy to spot the slate and stop cueing the tape at that spot. Bingo — you're ready to start, without losing hours trying to remember exactly where on the tape the footage is waiting. It ends up working like a chapter divider in a book. Imagine shooting a feature, with numerous takes of each shot or scene, and hours of tape to sift through, or returning to a tape from years ago, to try to find that memorable exterior shot (Figure 9.1). You'll be glad you recorded these digital reference points.

Another good trick, depending on your camera, is called blacking the tape. This involves running the entire tape, with the lens cap on, in record mode. This helps eliminate breaks in the time code, which is the digital "road map" that software uses to find its way on a piece of media. It looks like this — 01:45:30;20 — meaning 1 hour, 45 minutes, 30 seconds, and 20 frames. Most cameras generate the time code (again, the main exception being advanced, external audio decks which create the code). By blacking tape, you lay in a solid, unbroken string of time code. This way, if you need to "roll back" to check a shot on location, you don't end up with nasty time-code breaks (those mysterious blue patches of tape where the numbers "freeze").

In general, even if your camera has a feature that allows you to check your last shot, try to avoid this temptation. Until you know your camera backwards and forwards, you don't want to risk creating a time code break or, worse, recording over previously shot footage. Shooting slates will also help you to avoid this mistake. Good in-camera tape management will help you avoid a ton of head-aches during editing. Again, like white balancing, setting focus, and adjusting your iris, all of this slate stuff might seem like a big burden. But once you have some practice and a few shoots under your belt, you'll bang out these tasks so fast that you will hardly notice.

TIP 10 PATIENCE, GRASSHOPPER

Musicians spend hours in solitude, playing standard scales over and over again. The multimillion-dollar athletes we love to watch on TV spend ages in the weight room and in practice facilities repeating endless drills. And the world's finest chefs have a special garbage pail reserved just for their hours of inedible experiments.

Have patience, grasshopper. You will need some time to practice your shots, review your footage, and refine your skills. But you must be ready to put in the time: to stand at the beach for two hours practicing your pans, to stop your car at odd places because you think you can grab a memorable shot, to lug your tripod on every hike you take.

And you need to train your eye. Most camcorders have built-in mikes, so talk to yourself as you practice shots. When you make adjustments to the various camera settings, dictate the changes. Talk your way through each small iris or framing change. Then, when you review the footage, train your eye to see the difference, to pay attention to the slightest adjustment. Here's another good trick: Start watching TV with the sound off. I know, I know, your friends, family, and roommates will think you're insane. Too bad. Muting the sound keeps you from being drawn in to the on-screen drama, be it a car commercial or a prime-time cop show. Talk about what you see. Call it out loud as you see it and force your eye to absorb the details — the shots, framings, lighting, editing. I know, I know, now these people will *really* think you've lost it. Just tell them you're in training and laugh if they can't take the joke. Start a journal. Write about every cool sunset, campfire, reflection, angle, shadow,

and glint of light that you encounter. Then try to recreate each one. Train your eye, and your movies will grow, like magic (Figure 10.1).

Figure 10.1

TEN BY TEN, ON YOUR MARK

HERE ARE TEN IMPORTANT CONSIDERATIONS TO EXAMINE *BEFORE* YOU START SHOOTING. YOU SHOULD BE ABLE TO KNOCK THESE OFF WITHOUT LEAVING HOME!

1. Get Zen with your camera. Find where all the controls, menus, buttons, inputs, and outputs are located. Know where any and all of the accessory elements are (that little silver slot, probably on top of your camera? It's called a "shoe" and lets you attach things like wireless mikes, lights, etc.). Know that thing backwards and forwards.

2. Did you start your journal yet? Hmmm. Well, at least go *buy* a blank notebook!

3. With your camera turned on, run the A/V cable from the camera to your TV (hopefully your camera came with this type of output and cable). Lock it off, pointed at a stationary object, like a plant or a painting. While cruising through the basic camera adjustments (iris, white balance, etc.), check the TV to find out how the image is changing. Get comfortable with each major function.

4. Set up your tripod. Take it down again. Repeat until you can command this task with minimal effort. You may also now recite your favorite line from *The Karate Kid*.

5. Practice this same exercise with attaching the tripod plate to the camera and removing it again. Also practice popping the camera and attached plate into the slot on the top of the tripod head. This one can get frustrating, so be patient — and practice!

6. No journal yet? How about a sketch book? Try starting to draw basic ideas that you see. Don't worry about artistic ability — just jot ideas down. Draw the frame and place figures, buildings, and shapes inside. Add arrows to suggest camera moves.

7. Get organized. Is your camera bag packed the way you like? Is there a spot cleared in your trunk/van/backpack for your tripod? Are your batteries charged and ready to go? Have a good pair of headphones for checking audio? Microphones working well?

8. Get your gear on! It can't hurt to gather some ancillary supplies together, that is, if you're *really* serious about all this video stuff. I recommend a good flashlight, some duct tape (or gaffer tape), a utility knife, some work gloves, a permanent marker or two, a couple of heavy gauge extension cords, and a power strip.

9. Still not writing a journal? Here's a list of cool things to look for and to sketch/ write about each and every time you spot them: cool lights, cool shadows, cool textures, weird arches and doorframes, interesting camera moves from a film, great editing in a music video, sunsets, moonlight sparkling on a lake, rainwater mixing with oil in a puddle, stained glass windows, slick graphics on a sports broadcast, great use of costumes in a TV show, reflections, campfires, prisms, and rainbows.

10. Check your calendar. Video is great fun, but can eat up lots of time. Be ready to devote yourself to improving. Block out some "play" time to capture images and a bunch more for editing (this takes three times longer than any client thinks it will!).

SECTION 2

BASICS ▶

TIP 11
FRAME 'EM, DAN-O

The basic visual storytelling device that we employ is called the frame, which is the rectangular image that is created by the devices you shoot with and recreated by the devices our viewers use to see your work: TVs, movie screens, monitors, and phones.

The frame limits what you can share or show and defines what you allow your viewers to see or experience. It is both a result of older technologies (theater, painting, photography) and an exploration of current technology (TV, mobile devices, the Web). It is your window on the world, and it will confine you and free you at the same time. You will return to the basic rules and behaviors of the frame time and time again, so it will be crucial to explain and explore them first. (Warning: math concepts ahead!)

The frame consists of three axes that explain how this phenomenon affects images. The two obvious axes are the horizontal (Figure 11.1) and vertical (Figure 11.2), identified as X (horizontal) and Y (vertical). Since all moving images (film, video, TV, animation) exist as two-dimensional media (flat screens), these two define most of how you compose, or frame, your shots. The relationship between the two is known as an aspect ratio and is based on the idea that any rectangle is "X" number of units wide and "Y" units tall. Therefore, the ratio comparing the width to the height of a rectangle looks like this: X:Y. Traditional TV, and most

video, exists in a 4:3 aspect ratio. In other words, it's slightly wider (4 units) than it is tall (3 units). HD images are shot in a 16:9 aspect ratio and are therefore wider than standard definition images. Okay, you can breathe now. The worst of the math is over.

The more interesting axis is the perception of depth (or any diagonal elements in the shot), which is identified by the Z axis (Figure 11.3). Despite the fact that video images are flat, the illusion of depth (the distance between the frame and objects further from the camera) is a powerful tool. Likewise, arranging elements in the frame to form diagonal images along the Z axis can help shape your images in an artistically and aesthetically pleasing way.

You will explore both movement of the frame and movement within the frame as you move ahead in the book, but this is a crucial distinction to understand now. Any movement of the frame is essentially a camera move, like a pan or a tilt. And movement in the frame involves motion by any object, actor, animals, the environment (wind, rain, volcanoes), the background, graphics, costumes, vehicles, and so forth. Sometimes a simple movement of the frame completes the story. But often the most powerful choice is to resist movement, allowing the action within the shot to stand on its own. Combine the two in a memorable way and you will truly be on your way to video greatness.

Figure 11.1

Figure 11.2

Figure 11.3

TIP 12
THE TOP TEN

Okay, now you're really ready to get started. So turn off your video game, fire up your camera, and let's get to work. Where to begin? How about "The Top Ten Most Common Shots" (according to absolutely no official source whatsoever).

The most common shots used in film and video are as follows: pan, tilt, dolly, track (or truck), handheld, high/low angle, singles/two-shots, pedestals, crane or jib shots, and — here's where things get nasty — zooms. Each has its own distinct flavor, attributes, and limitations that can help your videos rock. Let's run through each one.

Panning pivots the camera from left to right (or vice versa) on a fixed point or axis (your tripod!). This shot explores horizontal movement of the frame and is great for shooting exteriors, capturing sporting events, following action (movement *in* the frame), and revealing information (an actor moves from left to right in order to open a door, for instance). Tilting is similar, but the camera rotates up and down from a fixed point, emphasizing the vertical axis. Tilts are a great way to reveal information slowly to an audience. For example, as new characters are introduced, you see them walk into the shot, and the camera slowly tilts up to reveal who they are — from their choice of shoes on up to their face. Using tilts to establish locations is also very powerful. For example, if your actors walk into a building, and you tilt up to reveal that they have entered an FBI field office, this is a different type of story than if you tilt to reveal a bank, hospital, or radio station.

Dollying and tracking are related, as each involves moving the camera along a line instead of rotating it from a single point. A dolly move traditionally involves moving the camera closer or farther from your subject, on a straight line. Dolly in, and you increase the intimacy between your viewer and your subject. Dolly out, and the reverse is true. Tracking (also called trucking) moves the camera past the subject or with the subject on a line *parallel to the lens*. While either move can involve placing the camera on a special moving platform (a dolly), and keeping the shot straight using tracks (like railroad tracks), the names are typically *NOT* interchangeable. Dollying moves the camera in or out; tracking moves the camera side to side. And here's the best part: You don't need to rent an expensive rig to get these shots. Anything with wheels that can safely hold a camera can work. This includes shopping carts, wheelchairs, tripods with wheeled bases, skateboards, furniture dollies, and wagons (see Tip 73). You can even give the camera to a brave (and hopefully skilled) operator wearing roller blades. So long as no one gets hurt and nothing gets broken, the shot counts.

This brings us to handheld shots. Like it sounds, this is shooting with the camera in your hands or propped on your shoulder (as with the larger cameras often used by news crews). Handheld shots can be very good for certain dramatic moments, to show the audience a particular point of view, or for shooting fluid action, like sports. Just don't get crazy — too much swinging the camera around and your viewers will get seasick! Some camera operators use a Steadicam, which is a device worn by the operator that simulates the rapid changes and fluid movements you get from handheld work, but with more exacting, repeatable results. A proper Steadicam rig is huge, heavy, and expensive, and it takes ages to operate one effectively, but more affordable variations and imitations have been introduced in recent years. Some shooters prefer using a small, affordable extension arm that can help steady shots and add balance when attached to today's smaller camcorders.

High and low angle shots are technically not camera moves, but can add great visual elements to your story. You can use a tripod to get high up for a shot or simply take the camera with you on a Ferris wheel, ladder, fire truck, or fire escape. For low angles, you can place the camera on the ground, balance it on a pillow, or lie down with it in a ditch. Just be safe. Don't climb on your roof and then tell your parents that I told you to! And be creative. Orson Welles supposedly once dug a pit in the concrete floor of a soundstage to get just the right low angle for a shot in *Citizen Kane*. In fact, the "weaker" characters in that film are mostly shot from higher angles, while the "stronger" characters are shot from below. Explore. Trust your eyes. These odd angles can add a ton of zip to your shots.

If a burger with one patty is a single, then a burger with two must be a double, right? Similarly, a single is any shot that only features one actor, and a two-shot (rarely is this called a double) is any shot that captures two. Singles and two-shots are usually framed as mediums or medium close-ups (see next tip) and are great for working your way through dialogue sequences. Most news is also shot using medium singles. A "clean" single is a shot that completely focuses on one actor, while a "dirty" single may include a hint of a shoulder or the back of another actor's head.

A pedestal move simply involves raising or lowering the camera in a straight, vertical line, just like what you would see if we were to step onto... a pedestal! TV studio cameras most commonly employ this movement, and they can be tough to execute when simply holding the camera by hand. You can try pedestal moves with certain tripods that have a center pole, or goose neck, that extends up and down, especially if this is done using a crank — if not, try playing with the drag settings to capture a smooth vertical movement.

Crane or jib shots involve securing the camera to a movable arm to capture swirling, dynamic motion that covers a lot of distance (or action) with a flourish. Jibs are smaller, easier to transport, and good for TV and video. Cranes are larger, sometimes as big as construction site cranes, and are used mostly for film. It can be tough to simulate crane or jib moves without one, as they allow for controlled, fluid camera movements that are repeatable for multiple takes. But this shouldn't stop you from improvising. Try using a seesaw, a heavy arm from a desk lamp, or some old dental equipment to simulate these moves.

And now we come to the most-deceiving move of all — the dreaded zoom. Why so much dread of zooms? Because every other camera move accurately mimics phenomena that you can experience naturally. Turn your head; you're panning. Step closer to someone; you are dollying. But it is impossible for us to zoom with our eyes. Instead, zooms are optical "moves" that get us closer to the subject without physically moving the camera, exploiting the power of the lens to change the size of the subject in the frame quickly. Watch a few amateur clips from soccer games and you'll see what I mean: tons of zooming in and out, frantically trying to follow the action or the ball. It's optical madness, it's not organic, and it's big trap for beginners.

Don't get me wrong: You can use zooms for dramatic effect or emphasis, especially if they are executed *slowly*. Slow zooms are often called "pushes," and they give a viewer the sense that the frame is slowly drifting closer to an important prop or actor, or gently coasting out from a detail to reveal more information. Just be careful: Quick zooming feels cheesy and unnatural and distances your viewer from the story.

TEN BY TEN, CAMERA MOVES

HERE ARE TEN QUICK DRILLS TO SHARPEN YOUR SKILLS.

1. Practice panning, tilting, and pedestal moves. Try them at varying rates of speed and in different locations, or revealing different elements in each attempted shot.

2. Get in some handheld practice by following friends around your house. Make sure to keep them in the frame, not chop off their heads, and watch for abrupt changes in lighting. Just don't flail around too fast, and remember to keep them in focus.

3. Here's another handheld challenge. Pick an interesting corner of your house, such as your desk or a spot in the kitchen that's full of objects. Take your viewer on a first-person point-of-view trip through this spot — let the camera search for something secret (like a set of keys or hidden microfilm). Focus on keeping things steady: Watch that you don't move the camera too frantically or whip too quickly in any direction.

4. Shoot a traditional shot of a person in a chair on the phone. Now reshoot the exact same action from both a super high angle (making the subject inferior) and a super low angle (making the subject superior). Note how the angle affects the story.

5. Repeat this again, but dolly *in* to your subject on the phone. Then dolly back *out*. Use an office chair with rolling wheels. Keep it smooth and avoid rolling on rugs!

6. Once again, repeat this phone call, but this time track from an empty part of the room to reveal your subject on the phone. How does this change the story you are telling? Concentrate on maintaining a smooth pace over the course of the entire move.

7. Get things moving. Try a dolly shot with the actor moving at the same pace toward the camera. Long hallways work best. Now try trailing the actor as you dolly down the hall. You can frame on the actor or on an important prop he or she is carrying.

8. Okay, Sir Track-a-lot. Try tracking your camera along as an actor walks down a sidewalk. Use a shopping cart, wagon, or skateboard. Scout for cracks and potholes first. Feeling adventurous? Strap your camera in and use your car as a dolly (see Tip 77). Hint: Friends don't let friends drive and shoot at the same time. This is bad.

9. Got zoom? Try to grab a nice, slow zoom in or out from a stationary object or person. This can take a ton of practice, and a lot of smaller camcorders have terrible zoom controls, like a cheap little knob on the top. If you're lucky, your camera has a ring control or a touch-sensitive "rocker" switch for slow zooms.

10. Add it up! Combining any of these cameras moves can prove artistically fruitful, but beware: Blending shots takes tons of practice and a bit of luck. So get going. Do as many takes as you need. Just remember to review your footage at the end of the day.

TIP 13 FRAME IT UP

Figure 13.1

Figure 13.2

Your next mission is to tackle the basic framings, the ways in which you'll use the frame to compose images, from the widest to the tightest, in order. Ready? Good.

The wide shot is the biggest possible — used for mountains, buildings, crowds, or sports arenas (Figure 13.1). It's often called an "establishing shot" because it shows the viewer where the story is taking place (see Tip 52). It's also called a "master" because directors and editors use it as a guide when matching additional, tighter shots from separate takes (or separate cameras shooting the same take of a performance or scene).

The medium wide shot (Figure 13.2) is closer to the subject but still includes the background or environment (picture two people talking near a picnic bench where you can still see them both from head to toe). You can also still see portions of the location or environment that they are in (a park or a campsite).

Figure 13.3

Figure 13.4

Figure 13.5

A cowboy shot is an old silent movie term, usually used to describe a shot of one person, from the knees up. Why the knees up? Because early film directors discovered that, especially in Westerns, audiences wanted to see the cowboy's guns strapped to his hip as he rode into town! I know several pro camera guys who swear they've never heard of this shot, but I'm here to tell you that it's legit. Besides, it's super cool to tell your crew that you want the next shot to be a cowboy.

A medium is a shot of one or two people, usually from the waist up (Figure 13.3). A medium close-up (or "MCU") is usually a shot of just one person, from the middle of the torso and up. You see this type of shot a lot on newscasts and in interviews. And, as you might have guessed, a headshot is a tighter shot of one person, basically from the tops of the shoulders up — in other words, pretty much just the head (Figure 13.4).

A close-up usually involves seeing just the features of a person's face (Figure 13.5). It's often acceptable here to see portions of the head "cut off." But don't be alarmed — this framing is all about the details. If the shot is *not* of a person and is just of an object, we often call this an insert or a cutaway (see below).

The extreme close-up ("ECU") is where you might see just an eye, a smile, or a tear running down an actor's cheek. This is getting really close, and you usually only see this in films and drama, not in news, comedy, or sports. For your information: Comedy almost always plays better in static wide and medium wide shots, when the action and the dialogue most deserve our attention.

Inserts actually describe two different shots. One type of insert is a close-up, but *not* of the human face — instead you see the details of an object (Figure 13.6). Examples might be fingers dialing a phone, typing on a computer keyboard, or — my favorite — a key being inserted into a door lock. The second type is a shot that gets inserted between two other shots, usually to fix an awkward edit or to show what a character is looking at.

Figure 13.6

Here is an example from a made-up horror movie, showing both kinds of inserts:

▶   Shot 1: Medium of a scared kid looking at a door.

▶   Shot 2: Wide shot of the hallway on the other side as a strange figure approaches.

▶   Shot 3: MCU of the kid, nervous, trying to stay quiet.

▶   Shot 4: (insert type #2) The kid clenches his hands.

▶   Shot 5: MCU of kid getting more and more freaked out.

▶   Shot 5 (insert type #1) A key slips into the door handle.

▶   Shot 6: The door opens to reveal that the strange figure is Miles, looking for the restroom.

The last common shot we need to cover is called a cutaway, and it does exactly that: It cuts away from the action to reveal an important element in the scene. For example, you may shoot a wide master, then several mediums of two characters who are trying to find a lost cat. Both the characters and the viewer hear the cat meowing, but the characters can't find it. You can then cut away to a shot showing that the cat is hiding under a desk in the room the characters just left. Bad news for them. Good news for your movie — you just amped up the dramatic tension.

TEN BY TEN, FRAMINGS

HERE ARE TEN MORE DRILLS TO BEEF UP YOUR SKILLS.

1. Shoot my amazing sample horror film from this chapter. Come on — it's only six shots; you can do it. For the part of "Miles," I recommend Brad Pitt or Matt Damon.

2. Shoot the cutaway scene, with the two characters searching for the lost cat. Use any framings or camera moves you want, but try to nail it in less than ten shots.

3. Remember that actor on the phone idea? Not again! Yes, again. Only this time, shoot a wide master and then move in for tighter framings to "cover" the scene in subsequent takes. Remember to repeat the dialogue and action as closely as possible and work from the widest to the tightest framing.

4. Set up a news desk for a fake news show — in your living room, garage, front lawn — it doesn't matter. Start with a medium wide shot, then cut in to an MCU of your news anchor. Remember not to cut off the top of the anchor's head.

5. Beginning videographers always seem afraid to get close to their subjects, and you need to get over this hesitation. Shoot a medium wide of a friend making a cup of tea. Find a spot to move to a medium. Then move in for a close-up. And when I say move in, move the camera closer. Don't rely on zooming in from twenty feet away. Remember that here it's okay to crop out a portion of the head for a true, effective close-up.

6. Snap off a huge wide shot. And I mean vast. Think Utah. If you live in a city, try to go to a park, public square, or balcony. Let the tape roll. Obviously something dramatic, like a blimp floating past, is great. But even the subtle movement of crowds can work. In other words, let the framing do the heavy lifting.

7. Cowboy up! You knew it was coming. Can you recreate this silent era standby using a friend on a bike? Or a motorcycle? Or, dare I say it, on a horse? And please — leave the guns at home. It's about the framing (cowboy hats optional).

8. Pan across a room full of people, maintaining a medium framing. Try to start and end your move on an interesting element, like a cool lamp, an interesting piece of artwork, or your main character (see Tip 66). Then shoot a few MCUs to cover the scene.

9. Get into position for a high angle shot (and I mean, like, rooftop high). Start with a wide shot, then grab two other framings: a medium wide and then either a medium or a head shot, depending on how far you can zoom. (Obviously you're zooming in between shots, to reframe, not during the shot, which Miles loathes). This is a great way for your viewer to "discover" a character in a crowd of people.

10. Pick five framings and three camera moves and make your own silent cowboy flick. You can use them more than once (mediums being the likely choice), but keep the pace up, keep things interesting, and cover all of the action.

TIP 14 FINDING THE ART IN cARpeTs

In the previous tip, I hinted that most beginner and intermediate shooters tend to resist moving their camera close to their subjects. You need to get over this tendency, as soon as possible. And you can actually have fun while curing yourself of this ailment. Remember, "fun" isn't just a four-letter word: it's the key to your success.

This trick is all about texture, so forget those outer space shots, fight scenes, and green screen setups. We'll deal with that later. For now, you need to get up close and personal. The camera is a great tool for exploring textures, forms, and previously unexplored visual landscapes. And where do you find these playfields of patterns, odd shapes, and weird splotches of eye candy? They're in your carpet, the nooks and crannies of an old blanket, the patterns on your grandfather's old trash basket. In other words, they are all around you, but you have to get the lens close enough to find them.

Make a list of all the things you can find that have some sort of interesting pattern or visual element. This could include tiles on your kitchen floor, the faux wood grain in a bookshelf, or random swirls in a carpet or the grill covering your stereo speakers. Now try moving the camera as close as you can to these details. Got an interesting line that shows up in your curtains (Figure 14.1)? Follow it! Finding tasty elements in your rug? Shoot 'em. You may officially abandon your tripod now — follow your instincts and follow the patterns and textures that you find while shooting handheld (Figure 14.2). Remember, the camera may catch details that you never knew were there; your job is to get close enough to find them (Figure 14.3).

What's the point of all this? You have two main missions here: (1) getting comfortable with getting close; and (2) discovering random patterns, strange shapes, blurry swirls, and captivating blotches. Sweep the camera across a particular element, or subtly dump the shot in and out of focus, letting the beautiful randomness that you've discovered blend and morph. You might use these abstract images to transition between scenes, to indicate an altered state of mind, to convey emotion or the passage of time, or as an interesting way to join two otherwise unconnected "traditional" images.

Do you have a few minutes of cool, artsy patterns to play with? Edit them together using a favorite piece of music. Add a voice over describing your wildest dreams or deepest secrets. Blend these images against a famous speech, poem, or the national anthem of Finland. It's not about right or wrong. You should be looking for ways to blend elements in a visually engaging way. And you should be having mad fun.

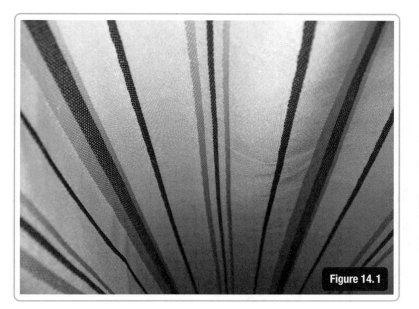

Figure 14.1

Figure 14.2

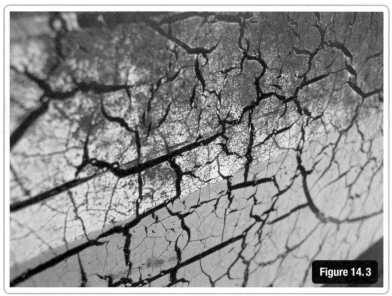

Figure 14.3

TOP TIPS FOR GETTING ARTSY

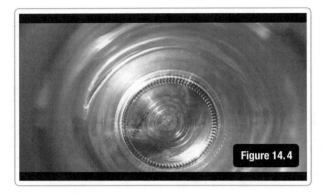

Figure 14.4

AS YOU CRAWL ACROSS THE LIVING ROOM CARPET, KEEP THESE TIPS IN MIND:

▶ Here's your chance to shoot out of focus, with the iris cranked open and with the white balance set incorrectly. Depending on the textures you find, these "mistakes" can actually add a lot of depth to your experimentations.

▶ Don't ignore patterns of light! Blinking Christmas lights, glowing neon, lava lamps, a candle flame, campfires, a broken fluorescent light that flickers on and off randomly, and other unexpected sources of light can become your closest allies in the pursuit of insane and interesting images.

Figure 14.5

▶ Do you have an old mason jar lying around (Figure 14.4)? Or that hideous green serving plate your Aunt Helen insisted on leaving with you last Thanksgiving? A bin of bottles ready for recycling (Figure 14.5)? A cheap magnifying glass from the dollar store? Stand 'em up and shoot *through* them. You'll find video bliss on the other side (Figure 14.6).

▶ Avoid camera shadow. This is the super uncool result of being so close to the subject that you actually cause your own shadow (or reflection) to fall into frame. This is tough when you're super close, but you gotta watch for it — it can kill your best shots.

Figure 14.6

TIP 15
VIDEO IS LIKE A BOX OF CHOCOLATES

Rumor has it that a certain travel company has spent oodles of money on a long-standing ad campaign that features… a garden gnome? And that a big-time insurance company pays a production company to shoot ads starring… a stack of bills with plastic dolls' eyes on it? Time for you to steal their thunder. And their paycheck.

To do this, you need to be able to make an average, everyday object appear both interesting and animated. Pick an object that you can easily place in various situations or shots, such as a stuffed animal, a pink flamingo, or a box of chocolates (Figure 15.1). Don't laugh: There are folks out there making mad cash because they can make a pizza box or a can of motor oil look like the most important thing on the planet (at least for thirty seconds at a time). I know two guys who shot ads for a fast food chain. For fifteen years they made cheeseburgers look amazing. But they had a blast, always had work, and got paid (and fed) very well. So pick your cheeseburger, or hair gel, or dish soap, and start shooting.

The goal here is to shoot about ten shots with your object as the subject. Don't worry about trying to capture the illusion of motion. Just look for interesting places for this mustard bottle, or tissue box, or pair of sunglasses to hang out (Figure 15.2). Focus on interesting framings. Pay attention to how one shot flows into the next one — how a wide shot of your object will cut against a medium shot of that object, for example.

How many places can a glass of orange juice teeter and still capture our attention? How many ways can you shoot a hockey trophy and keep a sense of joyous discovery when it shows up in a garden, a shopping market, or at a bus stop? How can various shots and framings help move this "story" forward (Figure 15.3) or convey a sense of emotion or tone? Can you get us to believe that a pair of headphones has superpowers? Or that a bag of chips is struggling to maintain sanity during the grind of a morning commute?

Figure 15.1

Figure 15.2

Figure 15.3

TOP TIPS FOR SHOOTING OBJECTS

AS YOU PUT THOSE CANDLES ON THE EDGE OF THE TOWN FOUNTAIN, KEEP THESE TIPS IN MIND:

▶ The unexpected is your ally. Try putting things where they *don't* belong.

▶ Don't worry about stop-motion or complex action. It will probably look cheesy, unless you get lucky or you really need to drop that taco off that parking garage.

▶ If you absolutely have to include movement of the object, try using a lazy Susan to rotate your object in or out of the frame. With a little patience, practice, and a sharp eye, you can also do this to rotate your product in and out of focus.

▶ Stop by an office supply store and grab some big sheets of white and black tagboard or poster board. Sometimes it works to see your bathroom behind the shaving cream can. But just as often, your shots will look better shooting against a neutral black or white background. This helps keep the focus on the product.

▶ Remember: It's the shaving cream company that's paying your rent. Make sure you include at least one "hero" shot featuring the company logo in focus and well lit.

▶ PS: Have fun. Just don't break any laws — or any windows.

TIP 16
WINDOWS TO THE SOUL

One of the first times that I ever played with a video camera came on a dark New England night when there wasn't anything to do and the rain was relentless. My roommate at the time could see my boredom meter rising, and rather than risk seeing me rush out into the freezing rain screaming like a lunatic, he tossed me his camera and said, "Here. Go shoot something."

Great idea, except I had no idea what to shoot. There weren't any actors around, no script, no storyboard. So he suggested that I shoot everything I could find that had eyes: posters, photos, book covers, old action figures. Next thing I knew — bam! Three hours had passed, and I had a clever little montage of just eyes: painted eyes, printed eyes, abstract eyes. All mostly shot in close-ups and "cut" together in the camera; one shot simply flowed into the next. Of course, I thought it was complete genius. He was actually a rather accomplished filmmaker and now probably thought that he not only had a total lunatic on his hands, but a total lunatic on his hands *with a video camera*.

What I didn't realize at the time was that this was my first, and one of my best, filmmaking lessons. I had taken an otherwise boring, ordinary series of similar objects (Figure 16.1) and enlivened them, using them as a theme to link shots together (Figure 16.2), completing my first video. And it didn't cost me a cent. And it won't cost you a penny, either.

So go find it, that obvious series of similar objects that you can shoot as a sequence, as a theme, as a series of images that are related only by their content — eyes, shoes, key chains, neckties, mailboxes, bumper stickers — whatever is interesting to you and your viewers and is readily available (Figure 16.3). Don't worry about transitions or fancy edits. Just shoot the whole thing in the camera. And let the objects tell the story.

Figure 16.1

Figure 16.2

Figure 16.3

TIP 17
PASS THE PUCK

Necessity, the saying tells us, is the mother of invention. So are crucial deadlines. A couple of years ago I faced both, rushing to generate samples for a job I was hoping to land. The gig was working video for a minor-league hockey team, and I needed original content to show them — fast. Inspired, I rushed into the living room, ripped countless pages out of magazines, and fired up the tape dispenser. In a flash, I transformed the kitchen counter into a makeshift hockey rink, complete with crowded bleachers, red and blue lines, and boards. I then proceeded to start tossing my hockey puck collection all over the joint (Figure 17.1).

I focused on capturing spinning, swirling pucks, smashing them into one another (Figure 17.2), and building puck pyramids (Figure 17.3). With blatant disregard for the kitchen counters, I kept slapping pucks around until I got more than I needed. This project ended up getting me into the top pool of candidates for the job, but, more importantly, it became one of my favorite videos. It's full of that dreaded "f" word: fun. And now it's your turn.

Using the concepts from the previous tips, find an object that you can set in motion, something that can spin, bounce, roll, stack, tumble, or glide. And don't hesitate to create an environment. You can recreate a sports arena, like I managed to do, or go with a simple all-black or all-white backdrop. You only need about five bucks' worth of large construction paper or poster board from an office supply store. To really nail this, curve the lower end up from the "floor" of your new "stage" (Figure 17.4). This will mimic those incredible, expensive cycloramas found on proper studio stages and it fools the camera into "seeing" an environment that stretches away forever (the curve hides where the "floor" and "back wall" come together at a right angle).

Next you need to think about the types of shots you want to use. I used a combination of moving camera shots, "snap" zooms and shots that emphasized the movement in the frame. For these, make sure you lock the camera in one spot (more on this later). Now the only thing limiting you is your own imagination. Remember, this isn't so much about still objects or objects in unexpected places. This one is all about capturing the weird ways in which one object (or a collection of them) can move. Have fun.

Figure 17.1

Figure 17.2

Figure 17.3

Figure 17.4

TIP 18
GETTING THERE

Here's an easy one: Shoot a friend walking from one location to another in less than ten shots. Sound simple? Well, it isn't. And no, you can't do one long hand-held shot. This isn't *Goodfellas*, and you aren't Scorsese. Yet.

This is a surprisingly difficult endeavor. Imagine a trip to your mailbox. You've got to start somewhere, establishing where things begin. And you need to get your actor moving. Most likely, you need to get him or her through a door (Figure 18.1), which implies at least one camera move (to the other side of the door). You might have to deal with a hallway (Figure 18.2), an elevator, stairs (Figure 18.3), a porch, or any combination of obstacles. The light may change three times before you get to the mailbox (Figure 18.4). So plan accordingly, but be ready to improvise.

Start with a shot list. Jot down the shots (framings, camera moves) that you need to capture all of the action, in order. If you're more visual, draw storyboards to outline your plan. Don't leave any gaps. The idea is to capture all the necessary steps (literally), without omitting any part of the trip. Obviously, if you live at one end of an apartment complex, and the mailboxes are three buildings away, you can compress things somewhat.

If the mailbox trip doesn't work, you can attempt any similar journey. Travel from the top floor of your townhouse to the first floor (for more coffee, of course). Or waltz from your front door to the pool in the backyard. No pool? Try getting a person from a bathroom, through a kitchen, and out to the living room to watch TV. Too predictable? Try the same exercise at your office, school, job, or favorite parking garage — anywhere that you can (legally) explore moving from point A to point B in less than ten shots. Focus on making sure the action flows from one shot to the next.

You can use this approach in almost any type of video, from dramas to the silliest comedies. And mastering it will definitely help you to cut corners while still capturing the necessary elements during those long days on location. Always be looking for ways to keep things tight. Trust your actor's instincts, but don't be afraid to do a little directing. And check each location before you shoot. No matter what the script says, there is always an easier way to get from point A to point B. And it isn't always in a straight line. Happy hunting.

Figure 18.1

Figure 18.2

Figure 18.3

Figure 18.4

TIP 19 PATTERNS OF PAIN

Checkered and striped and solid and plaid and even polka-dotted: Humans come in a wide variety of patterned and colored garments. This sounds fun, except when the people you are interviewing show up wearing a suit that blends in perfectly with the wallpaper, or their retro 1980s checkerboard shirt causes your LCD screen to flicker maddeningly.

These are the "patterns of pain," and they must be avoided. In general, look for a distinct contrast between your subject and the background. Contrast increases the clarity of the image and helps add depth to the frame. Put subjects dressed in light colors (Figures 19.1–2) against darker backgrounds (and vice versa); avoid combinations of fabrics and backgrounds that are complex (Figures 19.3–4) or clash severely; and avoid shooting subjects wearing all white, all black, overly bright colors (pink, yellow, pale blue), or thin vertical stripes (which distort into patterns called moirés). These are bad.

A quick solution is to rotate your camera to find an angle that doesn't feature the offending background, or you can ask your subject to bring an extra set of clothing. Top shooters drag portable backdrops with them, and you can echo this by investing a few bucks in some poster boards of various colors (stick to simple colors with no patterns). You can also use a sheet, shower curtain, or roll of fabric. The best thing about using poster board? It's cheap, easy to find, and can be quickly taped or tacked in place.

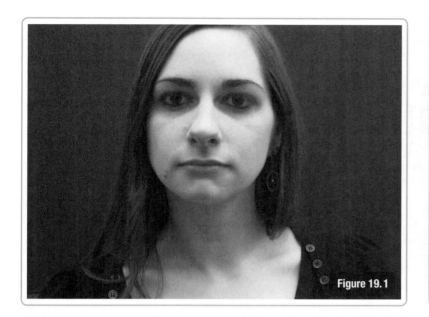

Figure 19.1

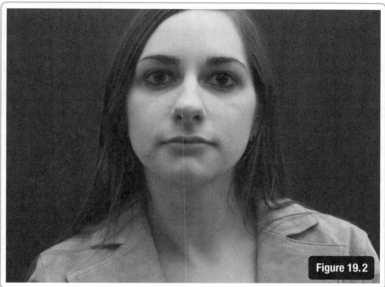

Figure 19.2

Figure 19.3

Figure 19.4

TOP TIPS FOR
SOLVING BACKGROUND ISSUES

HOW TO ADJUST FOR PATTERNS OF PAIN:

▶ Whenever possible, pre-produce before you shoot. Scout the location for simple backgrounds that don't contain complex patterns. Suggest clothing options to your subjects beforehand. Bring a light, simple jacket, in case your subjects need to wear it over their outfit (remember to choose a flattering, neutral color).

▶ Place simple, solid-colored outfits against complex backgrounds, and complex patterns or outfits against simple, muted backgrounds.

▶ Avoid matching patterns or colors: Don't shoot the guy in the striped suit while he is standing in front of a striped wall. Don't ask the local board of education member in the cream-colored blazer to stand in front of a cream-colored wall.

▶ Try some shots in which you purposefully have a friend standing in a pattern of pain. Then reshoot the same clip having made an adjustment to his or her clothing or the background. Notice any difference?

TIP 20
THE UMBRELLA DILEMMA

A few years ago, I booked a gig to complete a corporate marketing video, but I couldn't travel to Los Angeles for the shoot. So I hired a friend to get the shots and waited for the footage to arrive. This, of course, is when the true suffering began.

One of the crucial interviews was shot at an outdoor café, which sounds lovely, except that the interviewee was sitting with one of those giant table umbrellas directly behind him. The result? Yep. It looked like the umbrella was growing out of his head. Funny for you, super painful for me (I had to re-crop all the shots in editing). Yuck.

The "umbrella dilemma" is another classic trap for upcoming videographers. Palm trees, telephone poles, signposts, antennae, and other vertical demons are out there, lurking, waiting to sneak into your shot and cause unintended comedy. The worst part? If you aren't paying close attention, you rarely notice until you're back home, reviewing the footage, and your subject has long gone, unavailable (or unwilling) to reshoot. Granted, some of these results can actually be quite fun and funny (Figure 20.1) and, in the right context, might just make your video a hit. Just be sure it doesn't happen in your super serious dramatic movie or when you are interviewing the local district attorney.

Remember that the frame compresses depth into two dimensions. This is how odd combinations of objects blend in uncomfortable ways. Trust your eyes. If it looks like elements in the extreme foreground or the deep background might merge in a weird way, you need to be able to spot this problem before you roll tape.

The solution comes in two parts. One, you have to take that extra minute before you shoot to look at the less obvious elements in your image. Does an innocent office plant appear to be growing out of someone's shoulder? Is a light pole growing out of someone's head (Figure 20.2)? Is a billboard with an arrow on it pointing directly at your subject (weird), or away from him or her (subconsciously distracting your viewer)? Is the background color causing a problem? Are there too many variables (people, traffic, birds) in the distance that might cause an issue?

Two, change your angle. You can do this easily with an adjustment either to your shot (pan left or right, or tighten your framing) or to the placement of the camera itself. Often, by sliding just a few inches to the left or right, you can frame out the offending object and get on with your shoot, without falling victim to the umbrella dilemma.

Figure 20.1

Figure 20.2

21
33.3

Like magic tricks? Here's one that all the top cinematographers use. Take any rectangle. Draw four lines to chop the rectangle into thirds (like a ticktacktoe board). Use the points where the lines cross to frame your subject. The results? Pure magic.

Okay, it's not rabbits out of hats. But this simple, elegant solution to framing round objects (faces) in rectangular spaces (the frame) will save your shots and improve the quality of your images overnight. This trick is centuries old, has been verified by the finest portrait and landscape painters in history, and has made countless bad films look fantastic. The name for this beautiful insanity? The "rule of thirds."

Ignore what camcorders and common logic tells you: The center of the frame is actually the weakest point. Trust the rule, and trust your eyes. Take the horizon, for example (Figure 21.1). Our species has looked at it for eons, so we expect it to fall about a third of the way up in our field of vision. The same is true for the frame, and the rule helps you get it right. You'll have a horizon every time you shoot outside, as well as in most interiors. Adjust your tilt until the horizon is on the "horizon line" (the lower of the two horizontal lines), and you'll be good. Make sure your tripod is level: Otherwise it looks like you're on a sinking ship.

Figure 21.1

What about the human face? Since the eyes are the window to the soul, giving us crucial information about identity, intention, and emotion, and our species evolved seeing eyes at "eye level," use the rule to exploit this expectation. Use the top horizontal line (the "eye line") to place eyes when shooting a person (this works in almost *any* framing). Now place the center of the face on the left or right third, and you're set (Figure 21.2). Suddenly, the human face, that awkward circle of emotion and attitude, plops into a rectangle in a way that pleases the viewer and increases the visual strength of your shots.

Explore the rule in various locations. Try it with one face, or two, or three. Try it with objects, landmarks, landscapes, and tall buildings. Trust me; it works every time. And trust the rule. Frame your subjects on the left or right side of the frame, using the rule of thirds to guide you. Set eyes on the eye line (the top horizontal line), horizons on the horizon line (the bottom horizontal line), and 99% of the time you'll come out ahead.

One last thought about the rule and how it works with the frame. The upper left point where the lines cross is generally regarded as the strongest position in the frame, while the weakest point is considered to be the lower right corner (Figure 21.3). Don't believe me? Shoot two different MCUs of the same person, placing them in each of these two spots. When you check the footage, you should see and feel a big difference, and so will your viewers.

Figure 21.2

Figure 21.3

TEN BY TEN, BASIC BUILDING BLOCKS

THESE TEN EXERCISES WILL HELP YOU PREPARE YOUR MIND — AND YOUR EYE — BEFORE YOU SHOOT.

1. Jot down a list of all the possible locations where you can (legally) shoot. Note specifics about *why* you want to shoot there, hours each location is open or available, and any special considerations (parking, restrooms, power, lighting, space).

2. Make a list of all the silly, strange, unexpected objects that you can shoot. Start checking out garage sales for more memorable items for your videos. This can also be a cheap way to pick up an extra tripod or power strip, some whacky costumes, weird lighting devices, or a good duffle bag to store your extra gear.

3. Stuck like Chuck waiting for a bus? Think about the places where you spend your day as if they were a movie set. Where would you put the camera for each "scene"? Is there a spot to hide lights or microphones? What's going on with the textures, colors, and spaces that you are in? How would you move an actor through these spots in less than ten shots?

4. Make a list of your favorite products: mustard, shoes, motor oil, sports drinks, and so forth. Next to each one, write down one word that captures the essence of each product: spicy, comfortable, reliable, flavorful, just to name a few. Then jot down shots, framings, or camera moves that can help to express this essential characteristic.

5. Next take this list and expand it to include the locations, props, costumes, or actors that you can gather to help you tell the "story" of each product. The idea is to line up as many elements as possible that could help you create an actual ad for an existing product. These are called "spec ads" and they help new directors get noticed and get work.

6. Find an old picture frame, preferably less than six inches wide, something small enough to carry around. Drag it out every now and then and use it to practice framing what you see in your everyday travels. Be sure to explore the rule of thirds and the various framings, from wide shots to close-ups.

7. As you make your way through each day, keep a list of common objects that you could shoot as a series. Examples might include statues, door frames, street signs, trees, tires, purses, coffee mugs, and bumper stickers.

8. Spend an afternoon in the best camera or video store that you can find. Check out the tripods, accessories, cables, lights, and filters. Get to know the staff. Ask questions. Go to any workshops or demonstrations offered. Knowledge is power.

9. Tune your antennae to any local film or video productions that are happening in your area. Indie films are always looking for cheap help, and you are on a quest for knowledge. One path to becoming a pro starts with serving as a (usually unpaid) production assistant (PA). Yeah, you might end up making coffee and emptying the trash, but once you gain the trust of the crew, you'll move up, learn more, see more, and do more.

10. Get out there. Find a local film festival to attend. Take a tour of your local TV news station. Get cast as a background performer ("extra") on a big shoot. Bookmark a few cool sites that offer great independent video work. Soak it all in as fast as you can.

SECTION 3
LIGHT AND SHADOWS ▶

TIP 22
THE CONSTANT BATTLE

Ever seen footage that looks oddly orange or way too blue? Why this distortion? Video cameras see different kinds of light differently. What are these varying kinds of light, and how can you spot them? There are numerous types, from ultraviolet to laser light to candles to good old-fashioned sunshine. The two types you will experience most often are natural light and man-made light, which battle constantly to dominate the image. The key is to pick your battles and focus on one type of light in every shot.

Picture spending a few hours inside and then walking out into daylight. Your eyes need a few seconds to adjust, right? Your camera does, too, except that your camera needs your help. It reads most man-made light as "orange" and most exterior, natural light as "blue." This is because most electric light comes from metal filaments in tubes that heat various elements, like tungsten-halogen (or quartz-halogen). These types of lighting units tend to produce light that is closer to the orange portion of the visible spectrum. Natural light, meaning sunlight, exists closer to the blue portion of the spectrum. Imagine a snowy woodland scene, at night. Does it appear really blue in your mind? Now picture a cozy cabin in this setting, a warm fire burning softly inside. The windows glow with a soft orange light, right? Video cameras accentuate these differences.

You can avoid getting caught in this constant battle by remembering two simple steps. One, as you know, is to white balance using the light where you are shooting. A lot of camcorders have icons that might help you — pictures that look like the sun, or a flower, or some such madness. But be careful not to let the camera make these decisions for you. You should always rely on manually white balancing.

The second step is more involved. You need to be disciplined about not mixing light sources in a single shot. If you are shooting indoors, avoid including an outside window in the frame. Close the blinds or curtains so those blue frequencies aren't sneaking into your image. You can buy color correcting filters and cover the entire window (so the sunlight is *corrected* toward the orange portion of the spectrum), but this is expensive and time-consuming. Or you can drop a daylight filter on a theatrical light to match the daylight. The easiest solution remains avoiding letting more than one type of light source bleed into your shot. You may need to close those curtains, or move the camera, or even pick a different room. In the long run, it's worth the effort.

TOP TIPS FOR SHOOTING WITH FLUORESCENTS

BEWARE FLUORESCENT LIGHTS! THEY ARE EVERYWHERE, AND THEY ARE OUT TO RUIN YOUR VIDEOS:

▶ To the naked eye, there isn't much difference between most indoor light and fluorescent illumination. But the camera isn't fooled. Don't shoot your entire film indoors, under different types of light, *only to realize this mistake while editing*.

▶ You can sometimes replace traditional fluorescent bulbs with color-corrected tubes that don't distort your video image. This can get pricey, but is a great solution, especially if your entire video takes place in a building lit *entirely* with fluorescents.

▶ Fluorescents tend towards washed-out blues and sickly greens when they hit video. So either re-white balance under these conditions (to come closer to matching your other footage), or use this to your advantage. A little tint of green might be what your scene needs to convey emotion. Or the "cold" quality of a bath of blue fluorescent might help convey the mood for your shot.

23
ONE IF BY LAND...

There are countless possible light sources that you might use to illuminate a shot, far too many to discuss in detail here. What is crucial to examine, no matter the source, is the direction and intensity of your lighting. You'll explore both single and three-point lighting techniques next, starting with single-source options.

Direction refers to the angle of illumination, and intensity describes how dim or bright the source is in your shot. The best example to follow is a remarkably reliable source that is free to use, recyclable, and easy to take with you: the sun. The sun has informed the way we function as a species for ages, shining without fail from above us and at a slight angle. This is the key: above us and at an angle. If all you have to shoot with is a single desk lamp, or a cheap work light from a hardware store, do everything you can to mimic the sun, directing your source from above the subject and at an angle (forty-five degrees is ideal). Placing the source of light forty-five degrees away from the lens will also help unwanted shadows fall out of frame.

Shooting outdoors? Try different rotations of either the subject or the camera (or both) to line up your shot in conjunction with the position of the sun in the sky. Keep in mind that the sun at noon might actually look odd; it's shining from directly above (might be a good time to break for snacks). With either daylight or electric sources, direct the light so that the brightest part of the beam falls on the high cheekbone, below the eye. Of course, picking a more severe angle results in more dramatic images (Figure 23.1). Try lighting your subject just from one side, at a "flat" angle, parallel to the floor (Figure 23.2). Place the source directly behind the subject to create a dramatic silhouette (Figure 23.3). This can be done even with the sun, by simply rotating the camera until you are essentially shooting toward the sun. Is your image too bright? Simply walk your light source a few feet away from the subject, and the intensity of the light will drop.

Try each configuration on your own before you really need any of them in a shot. Make some mistakes. Explore different options and angles (Figure 23.4). Getting the light to fall where you want it can take years even for the best in the business. So get out there and get started!

Figure 23.1

Figure 23.2

Figure 23.3

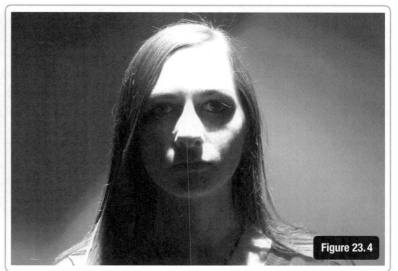

Figure 23.4

...THREE IF BY SEE

Three-point lighting is another traditional lighting setup, mostly used for interviews. As you may have guessed, you need three separate light sources to make it work. It requires a bit more patience, but if you trust your eyes and copy successful examples from films, TV shows, and YouTube videos, you'll soon have it mastered.

The three light sources can be proper TV lights or a combination of desk lamps and work lights. The main idea is to use their placement and particular qualities correctly. The main light is known as the key light (Figure 24.1), with "key" meaning that it's the primary source, the workhorse, and it packs plenty of punch. Place this light forty-five degrees from the lens, above and at an angle to your subjects, pointing at their cheekbone, just below the eye. Match this angle, on the opposite side of the camera, with the second unit — the fill light (Figure 24.2). As the name indicates, this light fills in the harsh shadows often caused by the key light (from the nose, chin, neck, and eye sockets, mostly). This light should also be placed above and at an angle to your subject, but producing a dimmer, softer quality (see the next tip to find out about "soft" light). You may need to back this unit up to lower the intensity, use a diffusion filter, or employ an accessory called a soft box to create the desired effect.

The third member of this tribe is called the backlight (Figure 24.3), and it naturally goes behind your subject. Aim for the back of the head, and you'll quickly master this element. The goal is to separate the subject from the background. This light is often the highest off the ground, should produce a sharp "rim" of light around the head and shoulders, and can benefit from colored filters. If your light isn't producing a lot of "kick," or if the subject still seems to blend too much into the background, you can spin the backlight around and actually light the wall or the environment behind your subject. Again, you might find it worthwhile to play with some colors here or add some texture (check out Tip 31), as long as you get some subject-background separation.

Try different combinations using two of the three lights. For documentaries, a combination of fill and backlight might give you a warm, soft image. Another trendy look is to combine hard, low key light with a radically colored backlight, which works great when interviewing athletes, musicians, and movie stars. I encourage you to set up all three lights in a controlled space (a studio, school, or garage) and try each light in different combinations. Then vary the intensity, color, and angle until you can produce both a flattering image (Figure 24.4), the main use for three-point lighting, as well as some interesting alternatives.

Figure 24. 1

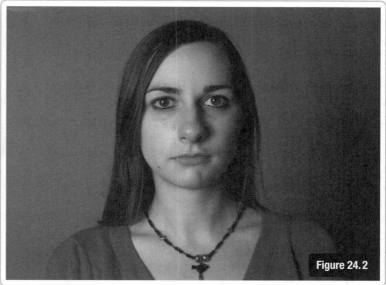

Figure 24. 2

Figure 24. 3

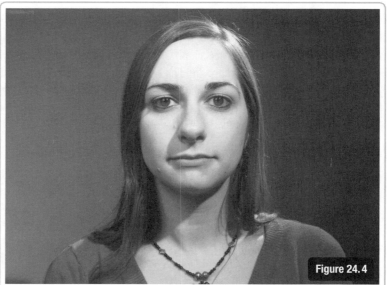

Figure 24. 4

25
THE HARDER THEY COME

So what is all this hard light and soft light madness, anyway? The secret to talking light is all about adjectives: sweeping, dim, piercing, brilliant, golden, blazing, glowing. These are all ways of describing light. And the two key aspects that you will wrestle with time and again are the hard and soft qualities of light.

Hard light is a bright, intense, tight, directed beam of light, close to the subject, that provides a ton of "kick," or presence, in your image (Figure 25.1). Think high beams sweeping unexpectedly over the horizon or a flashlight cutting down a dark hallway. Or picture that moment when the house lights snap on after last call. It's almost painful, isn't it? This is hard light. So is the sun at high noon, with no cloud cover. Too much hard light and you risk blowing out your image. But a good solid dose of it might just give you the exposure you need to see all the details. Be sure to balance the intensity of any hard light against your iris setting for a good result.

Soft light is a dim, diffuse, warm light, more distant from the subject, that provides more of an overall "wash" of light (Figure 25.2). Think about the cozy glow of campfires, candles, and fireplaces. Picture the welcoming warmth of a paper lantern by the side of a calm pool at night. This is soft light. Too little, and you risk not getting enough light into the camera, and your image will suffer. Too much, and your viewers might not know what to pay attention to in the shot. But don't worry. Big-budget Hollywood movies now shoot crowd scenes lit mostly with huge versions of those paper globes that you can find cheap at furniture stores (hint: pick some up). And there is a lot of soft, ambient light just floating around out there: streetlamps, neon, safety lights, reflected light, even sunlight masked by cloud cover.

What if you don't have enough cash to get your hands on a proper theatrical light that can send out a soft, diffused wash of light? No worries. Almost any hard light source (like work lights, desk lamps, clip lights, and such) can produce a soft glow. Simply turn these *away* from your subject and let the gentle glow reflecting off the ceiling or a nearby wall light your scene. Try combining these two in interesting ways to direct the attention of your viewers specifically (picture a hard pool of white light in a "wash" of soft blue light).

Figure 25.1

Figure 25.2

TIP 26 MARRYING THE LIGHTHOUSE KEEPER

In addition to intensity (dim versus bright) and distribution (direction and angle), light includes two more crucial properties that you can exploit to amp up your flicks: color and movement. Stationary lights and moving lights can both provide solutions for your videos. Let's check out both (and explore color in the next tip). Stationary lighting can either be technical (giving you enough light to make an image) or dramatic (existing in the shot for an environmental reason or because of a story point). An actor simply walking out of darkness into a pool of hard light can be an effective way to light a scene. Just think of the classic image of the detective roughing up a subject under a single bare bulb, and you know what I mean. Or picture a dark office building, black save for one small lamp on one desk in a window fifteen floors up. Patches of light can also help tell the story, as in almost every horror movie you have ever seen (the bloody knife on the kitchen counter is always under a small pool of light, right?). Picture the guy rushing from that office on the fifteenth floor to be on time for a blind date. He always forgets his keys in a convenient spot of light, cast by the desk lamp that he (apparently) forgot to turn off!

Moving light is also more common than you might recognize. Check out a carnival at night, if you don't believe me, or the front entrance of a casino, a movie theater, or a lighthouse overlooking a foggy harbor. Or watch just about anything by Spielberg: He always finds a way to work in a scene with flashlights dashing around the frame. Club scenes, cop chases, spy movies, prison break flicks — they all love big, sweeping beams of light (Figure 26.1), cutting magically across the frame. And what about our favorite rogue cop? If he's a real tough guy, the bare bulb above his captive is always swinging!

Figure 26.1

EXERCISE

TEN BY TEN, LIGHTS AND MOTION

BEST WAY TO EXPLORE THESE OPTIONS? GET OUT THERE AND PLAY IN THE LIGHT.

1. Shoot an actor walking into a stationary pool of light, at night, using two framings.

2. Find a colored sign that rotates colors or shapes. Use it to silhouette an actor and then shoot it again from a new angle, using the glow from this source to light your actor.

3. Shoot a chase scene in your backyard using only flashlights. Just don't get hurt.

4. Use a household light to isolate a table in your house. Shoot an actor either removing or placing an object in this "pool" of light: bloody knife *not* recommended.

5. Find a cool parking garage and use only the existing lighting to shoot an actor walking toward a car. Then re-white balance to see if the fluorescent lights can look more blue, more bizarre, or more washed-out.

6. Shoot an actor grabbing a late night snack using only the glow from the fridge (preferably when it's opened) and one other light source of your choice.

7. Head to your local hardware store and buy one of those cheap, silver clip lamps that people hang over their workbenches. You should be able to string the cord above your head, remove the silver dish, and recreate a detective interrogation scene.

8. Now go back to the hardware store. Buy a few more clip lamps. String 'em up in your garage and swing them in different directions. Use this effect to shoot a music video for your girlfriend's band, or your dad's band, whichever one is cooler.

9. Do you have access to a long hallway, lit by a series of lights? Shoot a long shot of an actor walking towards the camera, with each bank of lights turning off as she or he gets closer.

10. Ready for the big one? Recreate my amazing "late night office" scene. You'll need, um, an office building (or your dorm, or house, or apartment) for the wide shot. Then set up the "forgot the keys on the desk" shot. Be sure to turn the lights out when you're done.

27
CHASING THE RAINBOW

The importance of color in any image, from theater to painting to video, can't possibly be emphasized enough. Color tells you where to look, when to look, and even how to look at the image or a portion of the image. It tells you how to feel, when to feel it, and which characters are feeling the same way. It can dictate the time period, time of day, and the environmental conditions. And color can speak to you overtly or subtly about mood, tone, emotion, themes, symbols, and story. In short, color offers you a rainbow of tools and techniques, which you can spend your career chasing after. Here's how to begin.

Start by stopping by a theatrical supply store and picking up a small pack of gel. These plastic, colored filters are relatively inexpensive, can be used to color most light sources, and have been helping to shape visual stories for decades. The basic kits will probably give you a few blues, reds, oranges, pinks, and maybe a green or two. Some packs are more or less saturated, and some feature special gels for diffusing light. Don't worry about which pack you buy; just get out there and start experimenting. Pick up a set of wooden clothespins to clip the gel onto the front of your lights (avoid tape). If you want to sound truly pro, call them "C-47s" (it's a long story).

And don't let anyone tell you which colors are "right" for your videos. Green, for example, can represent envy, greed, sickness, or none of these, depending on the story you are telling. Who decides which shade of red symbolizes anger, blood,

fire, or terror? The important thing is for you to discover how these varying shades affect your image and what you like or dislike about the results. Be sure to note how various gels can dictate a change with your iris setting. Deep, dark reds, for example, cut out a lot of light.

Color can also be used in a simple manner, devoid of meaning. I like super-saturated colors for my backlight, for example, to help add a dash of "zing" to my interview footage. Other shooters use gel to light the actual background and give a little life to an otherwise dull wall. And color can also quickly establish a setting for videos that don't feature a huge budget. For example, adding a blue tint to your image instantly conveys a nighttime setting to most viewers. (Don't believe me? Watch a "nighttime" scene on any daytime soap.) Orangey colors can imply a different time period, while greens, blues, and even yellows can all convey a time of year.

And don't be afraid to break the rules. Any professional videographer will laugh at you if you tape gel over the lens of the camera, as this is not exactly standard procedure. But if you don't have a crew of electricians and a truck full of gear, and you need a particular look or effect, then why not? I've shot tons of stuff with my camcorder lens covered with gel because I thought the results worked. You should do the same.

TEN BY TEN, COLOR AND MOOD

READY TO PLAY WITH COLORS? GRAB THOSE GELS AND GET TO IT.

1. Shoot a medium wide shot in your living room three times. Change the color of the gel each time, but nothing else (camera angle, lighting, and so forth). How do the shots differ?

2. Set up a backlight for an interview. How does changing the gel affect the image? Swap out friends with different hair colors and look again at how the color changes.

3. Shoot a friend walking up to your front door at dusk. Then quickly reshoot the same action, but with a blue gel taped over the lens. Does it look more like midnight?

4. Different periods in history have come to be "seen" by audiences in different colors. Try creating a quick scene, using orange and yellow colored gel, to simulate a New York City apartment in the early 1900s.

5. Now try reshooting this same apartment, but change the gel to simulate the 1980s. Which colors did you choose? Why? Is this color change convincing to a viewer?

6. Colors can play havoc on clothing. Avoid lighting an actor in a green sweater with a green gel. Break out some clothes, a light, and your gel pack and find out which colors work under which lighting conditions and which don't. This will save you a ton of pain and suffering on your next shoot.

7. Double stuff! What kind of combinations can you come up with by placing two gels on top of one another? What if you cut some vertical slits in one sheet? Or circular holes?

8. Back it up! Ask a friend to sit in front of a plain, white wall. Shoot the friend in a medium wide for fifteen seconds. Then change the color of the wall by lighting it in blue. Notice a difference? Try it again with yellow, red, green, or pink. How does the mood change?

9. It's time to face facts. Have a friend sit for a close-up shot. Try lighting just the face, using a gel that is the *least* saturated. Does the gel improve the look? Which colors work best in creating a flattering image? What happens when you use a more saturated gel?

10. Back up a chapter, and reshoot the exercise that gave you the *most* trouble. By adding a touch of color, or a lot of color, can you improve upon the results? Make it happen!

TIP 28
BOLDLY GO!

What's the best way to tell ghost stories on a camping trip? You hold a flashlight under your chin, right? Why? Because our species is used to the sun coming from above us at an angle, so light coming from below us is bizarre and unnatural. If our planet was lit from within and the sun was under our feet, a typical sunny, spring day would *look* entirely different. Keeping this in mind, it's time to go boldly off into the cosmos!

Sound expensive? It isn't — travel to bizarre planets is possible in your own living room. All you need is the courage to change your lighting angles and a few unexpected colors. You'll need two things to begin your journey through space and time: all those dusty action figures (or dolls or stuffed animals) you collected as a kid and a coffee table. I'll wait here while you go rummaging through those boxes in the basement.

Here's the plan: Set up your figures on the coffee table to evoke a strange, foreign planet. Use blankets or a sweater to simulate the terrain and an upside-down ashtray as a UFO. Place your tripod parallel to the surface of the table. Light the top of the table in a weird color — green and blue work best. Using a *glass* coffee table allows for some really interesting lighting angles. The more severe the angle, the farther from our natural relationship to the angle of the sun, the crazier your alien planet will look. Shoot some pans and medium wide shots and add some sound effects, and bam! You're off into the outer reaches of the universe (Figure 28.1), or the edge of the table, whichever comes first.

Let your imagination run wild. Using tight framings, you can fool viewers into thinking they are in a completely different world. By adding just the right (or wrong) choice of colored gel and a few carefully selected props, you can set the stage for any number of adventures, from undersea kingdoms to a rain-soaked forest floor. Remember, as long as no one gets hurt and nothing gets broken, the only thing that matters are the images in the frame. The trick is to fool the viewer completely, using all the tricks at your disposal. And to have fun along the way.

Figure 28.1

TEN BY TEN, CREATE A WORLD

READY FOR SOME TIME TRAVELING? TRY CREATING EACH OF THESE STRANGE LOCATIONS, CONVINCINGLY, FOR THIRTY SECONDS. USE PROPS, BACKDROPS, RANDOM OBJECTS, COLOR, AND WEIRD LIGHTING ANGLES. THE ONE RULE? YOU AREN'T ALLOWED TO LEAVE YOUR LIVING ROOM.

1. Create the bridge of a submarine under attack.

2. Take us to the laboratory of a mad scientist.

3. Show us a foggy dock at midnight.

4. Walk us through a haunted forest.

5. Travel to the opening of a strange, magic cave.

6. Take your viewers outside a creepy castle.

7. Send your favorite toys to the hottest club in town.

8. Bring us inside a dark and dim prison cell.

9. Show us the deck of a starship or a weird UFO.

10. Explore a strange alley in a bad part of town.

TIP 29
TRUFFAUT OR FALSE

For a number of reasons (budget, schedule, location availability), major films and TV shows are shot out of order, and, in the most extreme cases, crews flip-flop their normal routine and shoot daytime stuff at night or nighttime stuff during the day. This is known as shooting day-for-night (faking nighttime) or night-for-day (faking daylight), and it can be a difficult endeavor or the salvation for your shoot. Either way, you need to master this approach to tackle the biggest challenges with smarts, skill, and confidence.

Shooting night-for-day is obviously more difficult. In addition to being up all night, you need to blast your set with tons of light to simulate the power and correct angles for natural sunlight. If you are lucky and have a huge crew (and a huge budget), this can be handled relatively easily. If not, get ready to get busy. First, scout your location to try and limit the number of exterior windows in each shot. Next, you'll need to obtain some big lights and blast each window with as much light as possible, keeping in mind that you might want to "color" these with daylight temperature gels (so the man-made lighting appears more natural). Other solutions involve shooting an interior door and over-lighting it so that it looks like washes of sunlight are pouring in as a character enters or exits. Just be careful not to get too bright, as this can add too much luminance and blow out your image. A few horns, beeps, and traffic sounds added during editing can help sell this illusion.

More often, you will want to shoot day-for-night, taking a normal, everyday afternoon and fooling your audience into thinking it's the dead of night. This is both easier in some respects (you're *probably* used to being up during the day), and more manageable (you are taking light away, rather than adding it). You will need to schedule some extra prep time before you can start shooting, but it will be worth it.

The first step is to black out any exterior windows. Almost any dark blanket or material works (think large sheets of construction paper), so long as you don't drape them near heat sources. Don't forget about the cracks under doors, the mail slot, and the dog door. If you need to create moon light, use blue gel and close your iris a bit. As before, light an interior door (that leads to a hall or another room) with blue lights coming from "outside." Couple this with a few key sound effects (hint: crickets) and you're good. Lastly, always look for the obvious adjustments to the script ("It's almost midnight") and the set (change those clocks!) to help push the illusion just a little bit further. Oh, and make extra coffee for those night-for-day shoots. Your crew will thank you for it.

30
THE SILVER LINING

Got a dollar? Head off to the local dollar store in your town and see if they have any of those silvery car window reflectors. You know, the ones that are supposed to keep the heat of the sun out of your car when you're at the beach all day? Buy one. You've just improved your ability to make decent images in video. Um… how, you ask?

Face it. You're never going to have quite enough light no matter how much money you spend on expensive gear. Even when you're shooting on the brightest day of the year, without a cloud in sight, you'll still find a few shadows creeping across faces. Here's where that reflector comes in handy. If you are using the sun as your key light and you need a little fill, position the reflector just out of frame on the opposite side of the sun and bounce a few rays back onto your subject (Figure 30.1). It's quick, simple, cheap, and it mimics the techniques used by the pros to bounce a hint of fill light into their shots.

Figure 30.1

Here are some other superb options to help you bounce the light where you need it. The next time you get a big package in the mail, save the Styrofoam packing sheet. These are usually wide, big, lightweight, and they work perfectly as bounce boards. Are you working a crappy retail job, but want to break into film? Your first step should be making friends with the shipping department and hitting them up for a few big panels of foam. You can also use panels of foam core that you buy at any office supply or department store.

Still not satisfied? Try wrapping one side of a foam panel in crumbled-up aluminum foil (Figure 30.2). This silver panel will produce potent reflections next time you shoot in the field. And the best part? You don't have to overpay for the super pricey professional version sold at most photo stores: This does the same thing. Just make sure the foil is crumpled up (but not torn) before you tape it in place on the panel — otherwise, the smooth, silvery surface can cause all kinds of weird reflections, unless that's a look you like, in which case you can make one side smooth and the other crumpled.

Other options include those silver aluminum baking pans that you can purchase at almost any grocery store. They're easy to handle, cheap, and readily available. Mirrors can also work, but I recommend these only as a last resort. Their reflections can be too hard-edged and too defined, and they can cause weird blemishes and streaks on the faces of your subjects. Mirrors also work best with less hard light, bouncing softer, diffused light in a friendlier manner (they're also handy when checking for vampires).

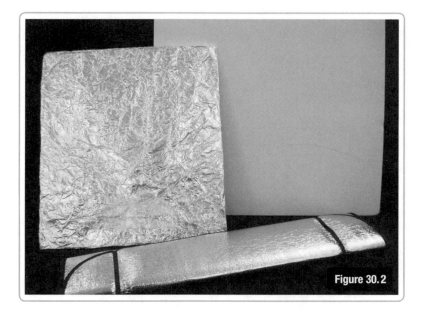

Figure 30.2

TIP 31
CUT IT OUT

Are you still unhappy with the results of your lighting efforts? For a few bucks and with a little preparation time, you can expand the possibilities for producing memorable lighting with textures, shapes, and settings (Figure 31.1). You'll also need a small craft knife.

Buy a few three-foot foam core panels from an office supply store. Cut a few random cloud-shaped patterns in one, and you've got what is commonly called a "gobo": a panel designed to break up the light into textures and patterns (Figure 31.2). You can make them by cutting out circles, slashes, or almost any pattern, but cloud shapes seem to work best. Be sure to experiment with your lights to achieve both soft-edged shapes (which appear as splotches of light or color) and hard-edged shapes (which produce a more pronounced, defined texture). A lot of lights may not have a setting for "hard" focus (where you literally see the edge of the pool of light), but you can produce a decent outcome by changing the distance between the gobo and the light. Play around with how these gobos create splotches of light on an otherwise plain wall, and you'll see your shots start to improve in terms of visual depth right away.

Figure 31.1

Figure 31.2

Are you looking for something more defined? Cut a series of thin, parallel slits in the foam core, almost like blinds on a window (Figure 31.3). Of course, this is the exact result that this gobo will produce, held horizontally (Figure 31.4). Turn them vertically and you create the instant illusion of light seeping through the bars of a prison cell. You can simulate door frames, windows, church steeples, barns: just about anything that you can effectively (and hopefully without injury) carve out of foam core. Just be sure not to place the foam panels too close to the light source. You want interesting patterns and textures — you don't want any fires.

Another easy adjustment you can make to the light involves copying another tool used by pros. Called scrims or screens, these are meshes of differing thicknesses, designed to lower the intensity of a light without using a dimmer. As before, you can buy the super expensive ones or you can just drag a window screen around with you on your shoots. The pros call these "singles" and "doubles," which describes the differing thicknesses of the screen (doubles feature mesh that is twice as dense as singles). If the light is too harsh, and dropping the iris down is too severe an adjustment, it's probably time to screen the light. Trust your eyes, make the adjustment, and keep shooting.

Lastly, to create a sliver of light that cuts across the image, the pros might use a rectangle of fabric called a "flag." These are meant to crop out light or create interesting shadows. Again, with a sheet of black foam core, these are easy to replicate. You can also experiment with creating different types of shadows and silhouettes, which always bring another dimension to visual storytelling that is painfully underexplored. Just watch that your flags don't get too close to your lights: fire = bad.

Figure 31.3

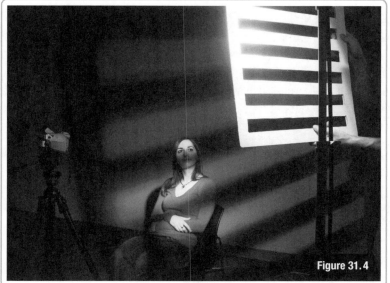

Figure 31.4

TIP32
DIFFERENT DRUMMERS

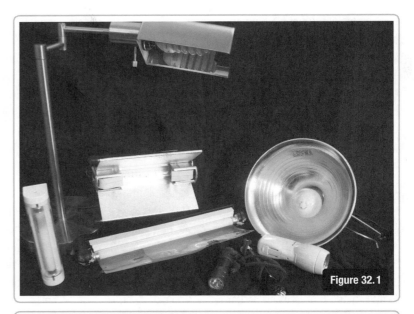

Figure 32.1

Think about the last time you walked through a shopping mall. Did you peek into one of those cheesy novelty stores — you know, the ones with the bad T-shirts, naughty board games, and the fake punk-rock stuff? What else do they have tons of? Weird lights.

Lights come in all manner of shapes, sizes, and colors: those little fluorescents, LEDs, globes, strobes, flickering chili peppers (Figure 32.1). It's endless. The trick is always to keep your cinematic eyes open to possible sources for new ideas (Figure 32.2). Pick up a couple of fake cop car lights, the ones people always call "sirens" even though they don't make any sound. They might come in handy on a film.

Use little fluorescent tubes to simulate the screen glow from a computer monitor. Tape a few LED flashlights onto an old army helmet. Wrap a dancer in a string of chili pepper lights for a music video. The only limit you have is your own imagination. And don't be afraid to shoot some stuff out of focus. Glowing, twinkling lights make for great transitions and artsy, creative ways to link images.

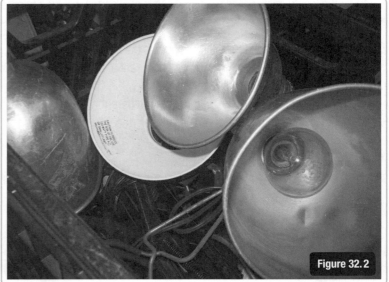

Figure 32.2

The two sets of terms that you should pay attention to when considering alternative lighting instruments are: (1) flood and spot; and (2) sourcey and hidden. *Flood* and *spot* refer to the overall size of a pool of light, with flood obviously being a wider, broader pool (Figure 32.3) and spot being a smaller batch of light (Figure 32.4). Some units will actually give you the ability to change this setting, while for other lights you will need to physically move the unit closer or farther from the subject to get the results you want. A light that is "sourcey" is one that strongly indicates where the light is coming from, including lights that actually appear in the shot. Flashlights, for example, are very sourcey: You can actually see where the light originates. Hidden sources remain unseen to the audience: Their *effect* is more important than their participation in the image.

Whenever I shoot video, I always try to get as much information about the location as possible. Are there lights there? What kind? Can I move them or add gel to them? Are they seen or are they tucked away? Is there a decent amount of AC power that I can use to power lights? Some location arrangements allow you to use their power; others do not. Be sure to ask first. Finally, are there any architectural beams, overhead pipes, or shelves that I can use to hang my lights? Be careful with pipes — you can use conduit, but avoid sprinkler systems at all costs. Always bring more than you think you need. Too much, as they say, is always better than not having enough. This is true for extension cords as well. In generally, get the heavy gauge kind, not the little brown ones that are meant for pencil sharpeners. And try not to gang more than one light into a cord, or more than three into a power strip. Otherwise, you'll definitely need that sprinkler system.

Figure 32.3

Figure 32.4

TIP 33
MADE WITH SOME SHADE

Take a quick look at your camera. Does it feature either a physical switch or a menu setting with the initials "ND" and possibly a fraction, like 1/8th or 1/64th? Ever wonder what this weirdness is all about? It's all about having your shots made with some shade.

ND stands for neutral density, which is a very specific type of filtering for daylight shots. Neutral density can either be found as an optical setting in the camera or it can occur as a sheet of gel, like a color filter. The big difference is that ND gel looks gray and you might think it's for some kind of obscure artsy effect, but it isn't. Neutral density is essentially like adding a set of sunglasses to your camera: It "knocks down" the brightest elements in daylight, without the quality of the gray color entering the image. In other words, it's like a pair of shades for your shots.

The big film crews can cover a warehouse full of windows in big sheets of ND in an hour or two. But you don't have that luxury. So on those extra bright days, when you can't close your iris enough, keep a sheet or two of ND close by or in your camera bag (assuming, of course, that your camera doesn't include this setting). Try slapping a little patch of ND over your lens, and reset your white balance. You should now be seeing the same colors with the same clarity, but with less glare and overblown portions in the image. This is especially key for white or light-colored objects in the shot.

Again, don't make the mistake of using this "gray" color when shooting a music video in a dark nightclub. It won't help you. In fact, it isn't gray color at all, but a specifically designed correction filter to help block out sunlight. So grab some ND, head for the beach and shoot 'til the sun don't shine. If your camera features an adjustable ND setting, shoot the same shot of a friend (a medium works well), rolling fifteen seconds on each setting. Have the friend hold the dry erase slate *in* the shot, indicating which setting is found on each section of footage. When you review the shots later, you should see the image darken slightly as you scroll through the settings.

34
GET A GRIP

I started learning about lighting in high school, then in college, and then on several professional shoots, but it wasn't until I learned a simple phrase randomly one day on a film set that I really understood what lighting for moving images was all about. The phrase? "Grips make shadows; electricians make light," and I have no idea who said it to me or if it should be attributed to any particular soul, but it rang in my head for years afterward.

Lighting, after all, isn't really just about adding light. It's about the fascinating, complex dance between light and shadow, about those interesting places where the light and the darkness come together. And it's time for you to take the same plunge, the next part of your journey of playing with light and dancing in the shadows.

You'll need a clamp to hold different items when "sculpting" your light. A proper grip stand isn't a bad way to go, even if you can only afford one (Figure 34.1). A grip stand is essentially a universal clamp (Figure 34.2) that can hold things like scrims or flags or other traditional grip gear (Figure 34.3), as well as things like tree branches and window frames. Yes, tree branches. Don't feel like trekking out into the woods to get one MCU shot of an actress looking towards a spooky house? Easy. Snap off a smallish tree branch, clamp it in front of a light, slap a blue gel on the unit, and bingo. You've got a character in a creepy forest

at night. And no one gets Lyme disease for the sake of one shot. Don't believe me? Try it. I promise you'll be blown away by this effect.

You can repeat this trick over and over with various types of objects, custom gobos, fabrics, shower curtains, anything that you can grip in place and shine a light (mostly) through. The goal is always to create interesting images for your viewers using objects to help sculpt the light, to help tell the visual story (Figure 34.4). Good grip setups also let you capture tricky shots (an actress alone in the woods at night) in a way that makes it safer, cheaper, or both to shoot.

In addition to some of the traditional grip applications, like adding scrims, screens, flags, or mattes (see Tips 48 and 49), grip stands can hold bounce boards, props, set pieces, curtains, signs, glass panes (see Tip 47), anything that can safely add a bit of zip to your image or complete a dramatic idea quickly and easily. The only limit is your own creativity. Try not to use anything too heavy for the grip stand or clamp to hold safely in the air. Need more support? Drape a sandbag across the outstretched legs of the stand, without it touching the ground, and you'll be safe and secure. Plus, you can finally tell your family that you have a grip on things.

Figure 34.1

Figure 34.2

Figure 34.3

Figure 34.4

TEN BY TEN, WINNING THE BATTLE

MASTERING COMMAND OF LIGHT AND SHADOWS CAN TAKE AGES. HERE ARE TEN TIPS THAT CAN HELP YOU SHAVE YEARS OFF THIS DAUNTING TIME LINE.

1. See if you can audit a lighting class in the theater department of a local college.

2. Explore as many hardware, furniture, and home decor stores as possible. Look for interesting kinds of units, placements of lights or unexpected uses of color.

3. Send away for a few catalogs from lighting and theatrical suppliers. Check their sites for discount deals, used gear, and product demos in your area.

4. Take a grip to lunch, or a gaffer, a director of photography, or a camera operator. Ask these professionals how they deal with light, equipment, and power. Find out if you can visit them on a set.

5. Find a job at a theatrical or film supply store. Get to know each piece of equipment, gel, light, grip gear, power cable, and accessory. Another perk? Employee discounts!

6. Crew up! The world is packed with low-budget shoots, most of which need your help. Get your hands dirty, your knuckles bloody, and your back sweaty. Best advice? Don't handle any gear unless you know it: If you have questions, find more experienced crew members and have them show you what's up.

7. Turn your garage, shed, guest bedroom, or basement into a lab. Fill it with weird lamps, power strips, and clip lights. Then play. Try as many setups as possible, stumbling on cool lighting effects or trying to recreate "looks" from your favorite films.

8. Organize a trip to your local community or college theater. This is easier if you are a student, but you definitely won't get in if you don't *ask*. See if you can arrange a backstage tour. Go to any workshops given by the designers. Volunteer to usher for a theater festival. However possible, get inside and check out their lighting.

9. Our species has been creating art and dealing with light and shadows for centuries *without* the benefit of electricity. Pick up a good art history book, or, better still, go to the best art museum within 150 miles, and check out how the masters handled light.

10. Modern art, of course, has embraced electricity in a number of awesome ways. Check out an art or video installation that explores light in a new and arresting way.

SECTION 4
SPECIAL EFFECTS ▶

TIP 35
ALL IN YOUR HANDS

Regardless of how your camera captures images (to tape, hard disk, or memory card), in-camera special effects are some of the most striking, memorable, and easy-to-execute tricks that you can master in your pursuit of better videos. A number of the tips in this section will be crucial for executing the effects and shots in the later sections. So, clear your head, charge your batteries, and get ready to rock.

In-camera effects are basically ways of manipulating the image so that changes that occur in the frame look magical, if not impossible, in the real world. They include disappearing or reappearing actors, props and costumes, jump cuts, double exposures, optical illusions, and wipes (where actual objects serve to create transitions).

The number-one rule for executing almost all of these tricks is to be disciplined about *not* moving the camera! Several of these illusions and executions depend on doubling up shots or otherwise fooling your viewers by not changing the frame at all. Your tripod and remote control will quickly become your best friends (Figure 35.1). Don't have a remote? Be extra cautious about hitting the record button, as even this seemingly innocent action can jiggle the frame slightly, ruining your best efforts. If you do have a remote, be sure to use it to start and stop the recording for each shot.

Also, be on the lookout for changes in your backgrounds. You'll want to keep any movement out of the shot; this includes trees gently moving in the wind, random

people walking through your shots, even reflections in glass. Any of these can be a dead giveaway that you are manipulating the image, either in the camera or during the editing process. You will also want to pay extra attention to actor and subject placement, as slight shifts from one take to the next can alter the illusions that you are trying to create.

Figure 35.1

36 JUMPING TO CONCLUSIONS

Jump cuts are an exciting, memorable, and effective means of visual storytelling, limited only by your own imagination and the type of stories you want to tell. Put simply, they involve tricking the eye of the viewer into seeing objects, people, and even environments "jump" from one condition to another, one location to another, or from one spot to another in (what looks like) the same shot. You'll tackle three executions of jump cuts: using a single subject, using a single prop or object, and finally the challenge of dealing with multiple subjects. Most of these techniques can also be mastered by creating the jumps as edits, but we will deal with them as in-camera effects, both because this is a crucial skill to master and because it's mad fun.

Picture a wide shot of the inside of your house, apartment, or classroom. A person is sitting at a desk, deep in the far corner of the shot. Then, bang-o! They "pop" instantly to the foreground, then "pop" to the doorway, then back to the desk. Some sort of technical wizardry? Hardly. These are simple jump cuts, captured in the camera. The trick is to lock off the camera in the wide shot: tripod locked down tight, no elements (like curtains, TV screens, or pets) moving in the background, and an actor willing and able to give you a variety of interesting poses (Figures 36.1–5). Simply roll a few seconds, pause your camera, relocate your subject, and roll a few more seconds. Repeat this process several times and your subject appears to "jump" around the room.

Obviously, this can be a bit unsettling and wouldn't work in a typical drama or documentary. But you see this trick all the time in music videos: singers jumping around in a totally haphazard way. It's entertaining, especially if you time your jumps to the beat. And it also can work as an effective storytelling device: How many times have we seen a movie about the overworked and underpaid lawyer struggling to find an angle in a tough case, poring over law books and testimony as the hours drag on towards dawn? Picture the same scenario that I mentioned above; add an actor in a rumpled, gray suit; and you have your stressed-out lawyer, his jumps around the room implying both an endless amount of effort and the passing of many hours through a difficult, restless night.

You can work the same magic in a long hallway by setting up a wide master shot, having your actor walk slowly toward the camera, and popping a couple of jump cuts during the journey. Presto! Not only do you shave off a few dead seconds from this otherwise dull shot, but you are able to express something about the character at the same time. Plus it just looks super cool.

You can use jump cuts as a character tries on 87 different outfits before going out, to show an athlete practicing 438 free throws, or to capture a young boy trying to teach his dog how to roll over. The possibilities are endless, the execution is fun, and the results are almost always glorious. So what are you waiting for? Start jumping.

Figure 36.1

Figure 36.2

Figure 36.3

Figure 36.4

Figure 36.5

TIP 37
THE MAGIC HAT

Now you have actors bouncing all over the room. Cool. But what about objects? Take the magic hat: an average, ordinary, everyday hat that has magical powers and can teleport humans instantly. Okay, it doesn't really have magic powers. But with your camera and a few well-timed jump cuts, it can sure look like it does.

These tricks are all about timing. Grab a friend and an interesting hat (Figure 37.1). Frame him or her in a medium wide shot, hat in hand. Have the friend raise an arm to put on the magic hat, and pause the camera just when the hat flops onto his or her head. Now, without moving the camera, have your friend exit the frame, but leave the hat on the chair, and roll a few more seconds. The result? It will appear to your viewer that the "magic" hat sent your pal off into another dimension (Figure 37.3). You can increase the level of amazement by trying to time the start of your shot so that the hat actually drops down onto the chair, but this can be tricky. You can't see any hands in the frame to hold the hat, so try using fishing line (Figure 37.2). Use this trick to have the hat transform from a cap into a fedora, to watch the actor(s) underneath the hat transform, or to see their costumes change instantly.

Figure 37.1

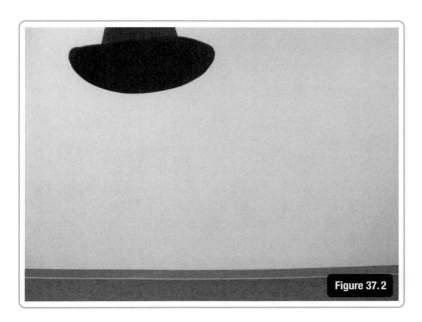

Figure 37.2

Figure 37.3

You can expand on this idea with any prop: a glass of orange juice, a light switch, a stapler, any object that presents a clear, workable action where you can make a clean cut. The "magic" elements are almost endless: actors can disappear, reappear, jump across the room, change clothes. Bottles of water can "pop" into the shot *just* as they are placed on a table. Another variation is the spinning chair. Shoot while a friend sits in one of those rotating office chairs. Make a cut at the precise moment when your friend fully sits down. Give the chair a huge spin *just before* you roll again. The result? The spinning chair helps hide the cut and implies that the huge burst of mystical power that sent your friend into thin air also caused the chair to spin! Good stuff.

You can now master a bank of "magic wand" tricks, in which an actor waves a pencil (or an umbrella or a wooden spoon) and the cat disappears, the sofa disappears, or a city bus disappears. You're limited only by your ideas and what you can put into (and take out of) the frame. Feeling brave? Teleport your actor from inside to outside, but you need to match body positions to make this one work. It helps to have the actors move in an overly dramatic way (like flicking a cape, jacket, or even their arms), which provides an action that will distract your viewer from the edit. Whether or not you shout "Alacazam!" when you pop off a jump cut is entirely up to you.

38
PACK 'EM IN

The third trick with jump cuts explores ways to put too much of one thing in a space that can't *possibly* hold it all. Students actually used to gather around college campuses and do this, cramming all of their fraternity brothers into a small car (this nuttiness, of course, was pre-YouTube). But now, with a locked-off camera, a remote, and lots of friends, you don't actually have to do the physical stuffing. Fool the eye, and the stuffing is all digital.

Lock off a wide shot of a car, with the front of the car pointing at the lens (use some tape to hide the license plate numbers). Then, using your jump-cut skills, send an endless stream of your friends piling into the car, stopping the camera every time three or four folks get in (your audience never sees them get out). Reverse this flow, and you can quickly create a cookie jar that never runs out of cookies, a can of soda that can fill 473 glasses, or a dryer that holds sixteen people, twelve basketballs, and a TV set.

For more comedy gold, just expand this idea. Remember those great cartoons in which a single hallway, with a bunch of doors, served up laughs as two characters chased each other from door to door, making impossible jumps from one entrance to the next? Whether you live in a fairly typical house with a long central hall that has just three or four doors or you have access to a dorm or office building that has a hallway with ten doors or more, the trick remains the same. Lock off your wide shot, pause your footage whenever anyone enters or exits through a door, and start jumping. These sight gags always go over better if there are a few other spots that people can "appear" from, making impossible jumps look easy. Look for clothes hampers, small windows, end tables, even couch cushions. Anything is fair game. Use simple jumps to hide the actors as they relocate, and the laughs will follow.

A more serious approach to using jump cuts is to use them in a way to convey odd jumps in time or space dramatically. *The Matrix* and *Eternal Sunshine of the Spotless Mind* each did this a few times, as have other films. Jump cuts in a drama convey a disturbing psychological feeling, or crank up the tension by quickly popping through the tense exchange of a suspicious package. The key is to practice the execution, so you can pull it off convincingly, and to use jump cuts at the right times, dramatically, in the context of the story. Otherwise, you may end up with some unintended comic results.

TIP 39
BOUNCING THROUGH BLACK

There's one more jump cut that is worth the effort to master. Better still, it's one that you can use in countless projects, from dramas to comedies to music videos to art-house films. I call it "bouncing through black," and it makes your actor appear to pass through the camera lens. Impossible, you say? Bah! It's totally possible. Not only that, it's safe, fun, and easy.

You can drop this trick into almost any situation, but it works best as a clever way to end a scene or to transition from one scene to the next. Start with your performer finishing whatever action is necessary, be it a line of dialogue, a song lyric, or a bit of action integral to the story. Then the actor simply walks directly towards the camera, stopping only when the lens is blocked by the actor's torso (or a coat, umbrella, or briefcase). The idea is to hit pause when the screen is totally blacked out (Figures 39.1–3).

Now comes the fun part. Start your next sequence with the opposite: The performer blocks the lens, keeping the screen black. Hit record, and have the actor begin the scene or the next movement, walking away from the lens to reveal your shot (Figures 39.4–6). Super quick, super effective, and super easy to execute: The main issues are making sure your camera rig doesn't get trashed (having an extra set of hands to steady the tripod is never a bad idea) and finding the best spot to have your video drop in and back out of black. I've used this one to "transport" an actor from an interior to an exterior in an interesting way. Remember that this version of the jump looks less like "magic" and more like cinema, so don't play it for laughs or "Ooohs" from your viewers. I've also used it to "flip" actors walking down a hallway, having them come towards the camera, black the lens, and then turning the whole operation around to have them walk away from the camera down the other end of the hallway.

You can also drop your tripod to waist level or knee level and block the lens with a prop. Think about my briefcase suggestion. Have one actor exit by blocking out the shot with a suspicious briefcase. Start the next scene with the same briefcase moving away from your blocked-off lens; only this time a different actor is holding it: same trick, different effect. This version is much more dramatic: What happened to the first guy? Did the "hand-off" of the briefcase go badly? The possibilities are almost limitless. I suggest doing a few practice runs before you need to make it work on-set. But I promise one thing: Once you have it mastered, you'll use a version of this jump cut over and over again.

Figure 39.1

Figure 39.2

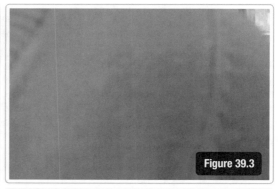

Figure 39.3

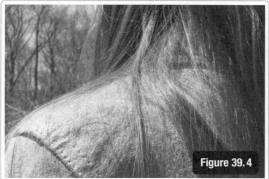

Figure 39.4

Figure 39.5

Figure 39.6

TIP 40
ANOTHER TRICK IN THE WALL

Directors and editors are always looking for interesting ways to transition between shots or scenes. And the basic cut, while effective, can sometimes use a little sprucing up. Enter: the wall cut!

Simple, easy to execute, and elegant, this transition provides a unique and interesting way to bridge two scenes together and is especially effective in films and dramas. The bad news? It requires both the videographer and editor to work together to complete effectively. The good news? If you are shooting a quick video for your YouTube channel, chances are good that you are *both* of these, making this technique a snap to master.

Here's how it works. Find a piece of architecture (a wall, door frame, chair, pillar, tree) that is close to your shot. Begin a gentle tracking shot that moves past your subject and becomes *blocked* by the object you have selected (Figures 40.1–3). Don't panic! This is the heart of the trick. Then pack up your gear and move to the next location or scene. Once you are there, repeat this process. Find another element to block your camera, start rolling and then…? You guessed it. Continue the tracking shot in the same direction (screen right to left) to reveal the next subject in this new location (Figures 40.4–6).

The key is to match the pace of the second camera move so that it is the same in both shots. Using this technique is an excellent way to "jump" across time and space in a memorable fashion, sending your character (and audience) from a rainy bedroom to a café near the Eiffel Tower in a smooth, graceful move.

The other portion of this trick that requires a little patience is the edit. The key here is to take the two separate shots and join them together to create the illusion that the camera has moved through the object (wall, tree, chair). Since the raw footage won't entirely match up, it's all about the pacing. You'll need to make your edit while the camera is blocked at the end of one shot and the start of the next, with the result being a length of time that feels natural to the viewer. Don't worry — it sounds harder to execute than it is. Miss it on the first pass? Hit undo and try again.

Figure 40.1

Figure 40.2

Figure 40.3

Figure 40.4

Figure 40.5

Figure 40.6

TEN BY TEN, JUMP AROUND

CYPRESS HILL WAS RIGHT. JUMP AROUND, PEOPLE! TRY TO MASTER EACH OF THESE JUMP CUTS CONVINCINGLY. PAY ATTENTION TO PACE, TIMING, AND LOCATION (WHERE OBJECTS AND PEOPLE APPEAR ON-SCREEN).

1. Lock off your camera and pop some basic jump cuts of one person in one room. Have the subject find as many spots to sit or stand as possible in a single framing.

2. Use jump cuts to have an actor bounce through black.

3. Use the wall cut to move from one interior location to another.

4. Use the wall cut to move from an interior location to an exterior.

5. Shoot an actor moving down a long hallway. Use jump cuts to shorten the trip.

6. Get cartoony! Find a hallway with lots of doors and use jump cuts to create a comic chase that defies the laws of physics.

7. Shoot a jump cut using a moving object, like a mysterious briefcase.

8. Explore the magic hat jump cut by making a friend "disappear." Hint: Using an odd or bizarre hat helps sell the "magic" part of this one.

9. When is a soda can not a soda can? When your friend takes a sip and puts the can down on a counter or table, and it instantly disappears. Make sure you cut at the right time!

10. Remember *I Dream of Jeannie*? That show was the king (the queen?) of jump cuts! Try a little genie magic by making other actors in the shot disappear as your leading lady simply nods her head (she should nod genie-like, of course).

TIP 41
WHIP IT GOOD

Another exciting jump cut is the two-part technique called a whip pan. You've seen it countless times on prime-time TV dramas, in fight scenes, and for exaggerated reactions in broad comedies. You'll need a bit of practice with this one, as it involves quickly whipping the camera to the side. You'll need to find the sweet spot where the whip is effective, but not so severe that it throws off your audience. Here's the way it works.

Part one begins as a traditional shot, covering a scene with a normal framing, but then quickly whipping the camera to one side, causing your image to blur. You'll find that handheld shots quickly lend themselves to executing this trick, as you need to rotate at the waist to achieve the desired look, but you can pull it off from a tripod if your pan and tilt controls are relatively loose.

Part two involves a similar move, only this one is a bit more difficult to get right because it involves whipping the camera in the same direction as for part one, but coming to rest on the framing you want. This can take a few tries, as you need to end your framing with the subject in the shot, hopefully in a spot that is compositionally satisfying to the eye. Not easy. I suggest avoiding whipping into tighter framings because this increases the difficulty level. Stick to mediums and medium-wide shots for this move.

This effect should occur mostly in the camera. You need to work the timing, so you stop recording as you are whipping out and start recording during the whip in for the second shot. The effect comes together during the edit when you join the two blurred portions, creating the illusion that the audience is seeing one swirled camera move. The whip dramatically launches the shot from one location, or point of view, to another. But to nail it, you need to hit start and stop at roughly the right spots in the whip.

Get ready to practice this one numerous times and to execute several takes on-set to get it right. Luckily, it's easy to practice in your own place before trying it during shooting. This trick is particularly effective in those moments when a character notices something significant out of the frame or when you need to move the story along quickly in a "flashy" fashion. It's also great for increasing comedic effect (especially for an exaggerated reaction by one of your characters) and for stunts (see Tips 81 and 82).

TIP 42
MAN IN THE MIRROR

My students frequently ask about mirror shots, trying to uncover the big secret behind pulling off this technique. Found mostly in dramas, mirror shots give audiences a unique insight into particular characters, showing us an intimate moment from their private world. How many times have you seen the haggard protagonist at the end of his rope gazing intently in the bathroom mirror, razor in hand, debating whether to end it all or to stand and fight? It can be a very effective shot (Figure 42.1).

And, with a little trial and error, it can be a very manageable shot as well. Bathrooms vary so much in size, shape, color, and layout that one solution won't solve every problem. Laying out a simple, foolproof approach for everyone is almost impossible, except to say that the key, obviously, is to avoid including camera reflection in your shot. Camera reflection is what it sounds like: the unintended reflection of the camera or the crew in a shot. This dogs us in a huge variety of situations, with reflections sneaking in from windows, storefronts, panels of cars, shiny surfaces, and mirrors.

Figure 42.1

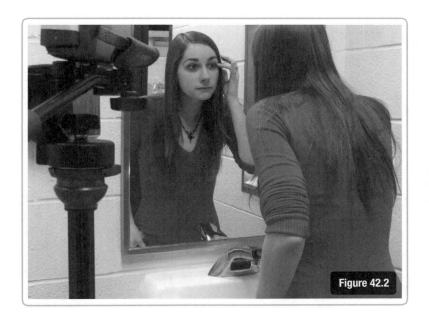

Figure 42.2

Figure 42.3

For mirror shots in bathrooms, the key is to start with your camera *reflected*. Then rotate to whichever side allows for the most room, watching your LCD screen (or external monitor) until the camera slips out of the frame. You should find that a forty-five-degree angle is about right, keeping you out of the shot and still giving you enough wiggle room to get the framing that you want (Figures 42.2–3). For more complicated environments, like a scene in a backstage dressing room of a theater, you can use creative placement of coatracks, furniture, extras, and such to hide your camera position. For more advanced situations, you may need to build a small set piece with either a one-way mirror or a subtle slot cut into the piece to allow you to get the shot.

When shooting in locations with a lot of reflective surfaces, you must pay extra attention to those corners of the frame where a camera reflection can prove deadly. The Web is full of sites that call out mistakes in movies, and cameras or crew reflected in shots are an all-too-common error. Never easy to spot, try to avoid these gaffes on-set (not when you are in the editing room). Again, look out for trees, mailboxes, bus stops, or actors that you can use to shield these reflections from creeping into your shots.

TIP 43
JOLLY GIANTS

You already know how characters shot from higher angles appear "weak" and those shot from below appear "strong" (Tip 12), but now we're going to take this concept a giant step further. The best part? We'll use some optical trickery to master this illusion, bypassing the need for costly digital manipulations.

The bad news about the video frame is that it's a two-dimensional medium, thus limiting our ability to manipulate the space within. The good news is that a technique called forced perspective can actually exploit this limitation to our benefit and to the delight of the audience. Forced perspective involves tricking the eye into seeing something that is technically impossible, changing the perspective of people or objects to achieve a special effect. In this case, we'll create giants out of ordinary folks (Figure 43.1).

Figure 43.1

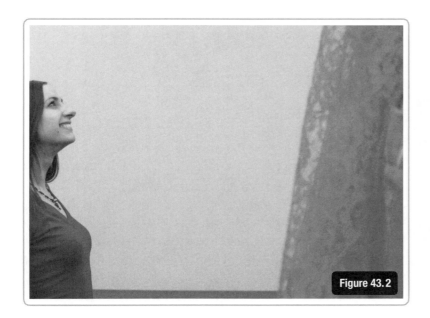

Figure 43.2

Figure 43.3

You'll need two actors for this one. Doesn't matter what size, as the biggest friend you can find is about to be dwarfed by the smallest person you've ever met (Figure 43.2). Place one actor, your small friend, for example, right next to the camera, so she is only seen from about the knees to the middle of her torso. She should be facing toward the right of the screen. Then put your big buddy about twenty-five feet from the lens, facing left, and framed from the waist up. With her knees out of the shot, have this actor kneel down (you may want to use a pillow if you are shooting on a hard surface), and look up and across the frame at about a forty-five-degree angle (Figure 43.3).

If your big actor gets her eye line right, the illusion should start to take shape: Your smaller friend should appear to be about sixty feet tall, dwarfing the supposedly larger actor. This is forced perspective in full effect. The illusion occurs because the eyes of the viewer assume that the two actors are facing directly across from one another, not spaced far apart: We are taking full advantage of our two-dimensional world.

To push this illusion even further, get hold of two versions of a single prop, such as a regular pencil and one of those giant novelty pencils. Or make two "identical" treasure maps (one the size of a note card, the other 11 x 17 inches). Have the "giant" place the tiny version of the prop at her feet, and then have your tiny person (your big actor buddy) pick up the huge version. This may require a few takes, as neither the actors nor the props can cross the imaginary line dividing the frame in half. This would ruin the illusion of forced perspective.

Check out the giant scenes from Tim Burton's *Big Fish*, which captured this in-camera effect beautifully, or similar scenes from *Eternal Sunshine of the Spotless Mind*, in which big Jim Carrey romps around like a four-year-old under a huge version of a kitchen table. Then grab two friends, two oddly sized props, and make it happen!

TIP 44
SMOOTH AS SILK

Another popular question from my students involves how to grab green-screen shots properly. The availability of affordable green-screen kits has made this formerly daunting endeavor not only more manageable, but tons of fun. Before you start, make sure your software has the capacity to render this effect. Final Cut, for example, does a great job with green-screen shots. Your software may refer to this as chroma, keying, or background deletion, all of which are essentially the same thing. The trick is to capture uniform visual information that can be easily recognized and eliminated.

Chroma or key effects used to be done with a blue background. But the digital green you see so often now is a better choice. This green rarely occurs naturally (eye color, fabrics), can be easily identified by the computer (your precious shots, after all, are only pixels to the computer), and leaves less of an annoying glow around your subject.

The secret is to shoot against a smooth, uniform background, be it green, blue, or another color. You can rent an expensive green-screen stage, buy a green-screen kit, or paint an unused wall in your basement. You can spring for the pricey green that is considered to be accurate by the pros or match it with a cheaper green from a hardware store. What's important is to create a smooth, evenly lit surface that presents the computer with uniform information (Figures 44.1–2). Avoid textures, light switches, outlets, scratches, or subtle patterns (like brush strokes). Give your kit a chance to air out, preferably hung in place to let the wrinkles even out. And you'll want to get this surface to "pop" with a wash of smooth, even, diffuse, white light. Avoid any gels and any "edging," areas where you can see the edge of the pool of light. The goal is a smooth, even wash of white light across the green surface.

The next step is to avoid shadows on the backdrop, as these will also pose a challenge to the computer as it tries to "read" the wall of green. Make sure your actors are at least four feet in front of the screen, so that any shadows will fall behind them on the floor and not on your backdrop. You almost need to think of green-screen shots as two separate lighting challenges: Hit the backdrop with a nice even wash, and light your subject theatrically, keeping shadows off the screen.

Keeping your framings under control can also minimize headaches. By staying with mediums and not showing feet, you avoid having to work against a green wall *and* a green floor. If you *do* need to see the full figure in the frame, pick up a few green sheets of cheap tagboard and some soft, disposable hospital booties. Green tagboard these days is close to the digital green of most professional backdrops, and the booties will prevent you from dragging dirt on the surface or scraping it up, causing irregularities that won't delete cleanly. Lastly, be sure to shoot *and edit* some short practice footage before you head out to

complete your sci-fi masterpiece. You'll want to be confident that your surface, lighting, and framings all work smoothly together. Oh, and be sure to schedule in a shoot to get the backgrounds that you will use to replace the green screen deleted by your software. Be sure to match the camera angle(s), and make sure that you shoot the backgrounds in wider framings than you think you need.

Figure 44.1

Figure 44.2

TIP 45
GLITCHES IN THE MATRIX

I realize that overhead projectors can be a little pricey, but if there is any way that you can afford to pick one up or borrow one from school, work, or a friend, you can crank out loads of cool special effects, textures, and lighting phenomena (Figures 45.1–2). And, like a lot of these tips, you are only limited by the scope of your own imagination. Here are a few of my favorite projector tricks.

Drop a projector onto the floor, shoot it upwards at your subject, dim the lights in the room, and lock off a tight close-up, featuring the face of your actor. This allows you not only to explore weird and wonderful textures, but to fake the glow of a computer screen. Hook your projector up to a computer, and you can show a simple word processing program across the face of your actor (Figure 45.3), making for an intense, on-screen moment (especially if you configure the projector to reverse the image, so the words maintain the proper orientation for your character). Or you can just shoot the raw "blue" from the projector (without hooking it up to an external source) to fake a computer glow. Feeling really inventive? Grab some cardboard, cut out a rectangle (the "computer screen"), and shoot the blue glow through this space to complete the illusion.

Remember your wacky, artsy textures from Tip 14? How about projecting these weird shapes and colors onto the singer in your friend's rock band? This adds interesting textures to a music video and doesn't involve any copyright issues.

Feeling really artsy? Hook up a second camera, run it through the projector, and shoot this double exposure of the singer, projected onto him- or herself.

Stuck for a location? Try projecting a pre-shot background into your image. Hollywood ran this trick for years by having a crew shoot backwards from a moving car and then projecting this footage behind a pair of actors sitting in a mock-up of a car in a studio. This can look corny, of course, but it does eliminate the more dangerous aspects of having actors talk and drive at the same time and also increases the ability to record the dialogue cleanly. You can rear-project these images using a simple white sheet or project them from the front, taking care to employ the two-step lighting process that you used for green-screen shots (no shadows, subjects lit separately).

For a really bizarre shot, have your actors turn ninety degrees from the projected image, causing only half of their face to light up. Shoot this in an extremely dark environment (be it a studio or your living room) for a pronounced result. Projectors also enable you to fake things like cop car lights or a scene in a nightclub. You can also use projectors pointing towards the camera to fake a scene of characters sitting in a movie theater (Figure 45.4). This is much cheaper than renting a whole movie theater. Trust me.

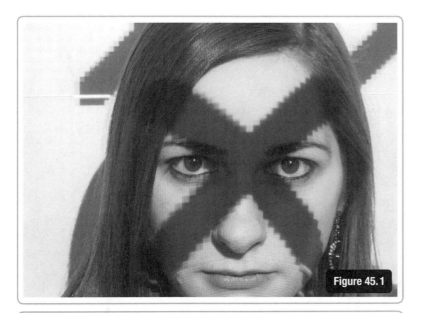

Figure 45.1

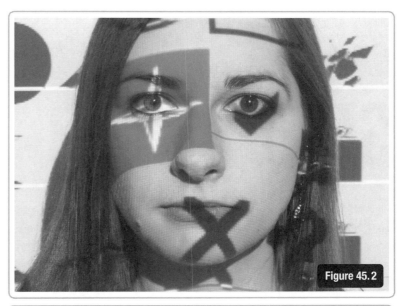

Figure 45.2

Figure 45.3

Figure 45.4

TIP46
SMOKE AND THE WATER

There are numerous memorable effects for water and fire that you can pull off safely, cheaply, and quickly. Just remember: As is the case anytime you are shooting, keep things safe, do not endanger your cast or crew, and try not to break any laws or, you know, blow stuff up. Ready to get wet? Good. Let's dive in.

Here's a simple trick for getting effective shots of light reflecting off the water onto the face(s) of your character(s). And you don't have to rent a rowboat to pull this off. All you need is one of those aluminum baking pans (Figure 46.1), the kind that most people buy to cook a turkey in, and some water. Fill the baking pan about half full with water, and shoot a light down into the pan. By framing up on your actor's face and gently shaking the pan back and forth, you should see these "waves" reflected onto your actor's face. Drop a blue light over your source, and it's the same effect at night. It's helpful here to shoot against a solid black background and to close your iris a touch. You can add a few key sound effects during editing to seal the deal.

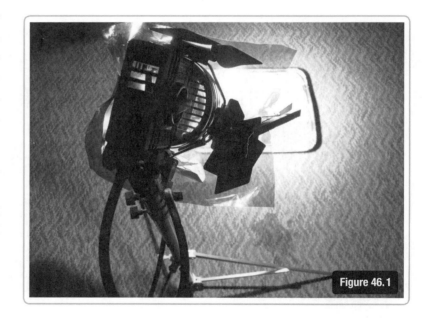

Figure 46.1

Fire effects are another memorable trick, and can be achieved without the dangers of shooting near real flames. Set up your shot as before, framed on the face of the actor against a solid black background. Place a light as low as you can and cover the source with red, orange, or yellow gel. Wearing heat-resistant gloves, simply wiggle your fingers in front of the light (and out of the shot!). Try different speeds and finger combinations to simulate the glow of flames (Figure 46.2). For a more elaborate effect, rotate colored gels in different combinations, sending splinters of red, orange, or yellow into the shot. You'll obviously want to take care not to burn your fingers, which isn't too tough. Or use some wooden spoons for the flicker. Your set will be a thousand times safer.

This effect can also be repeated on location and often *must* be, since certain parks and even campsites don't allow open flames. The key is to simulate the glow, not the actual flames. Adding a sound effect (or even creating one — see Tip 91) will do wonders for pulling off this trick. You can also wire up a "flicker box." This is what the professionals use to complete this same effect. It's essentially a box that sends random electric signals to a few low-wattage lights, thus eliminating the need to wiggle your fingers for the entire shoot. Need a truly pro version? Check local theatrical supply stores to rent a flicker box.

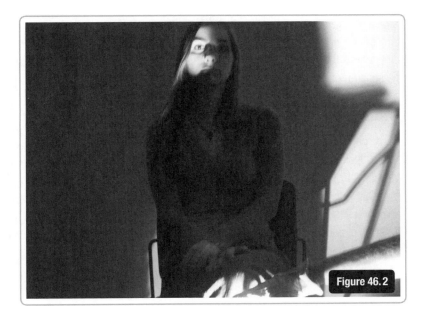

Figure 46.2

TIP 47
GHOSTS IN THE MACHINE

There are a number of cool effects that you can master using a simple pane of glass, from ghosts to floating heads and more. But for all of them, you will need to hold the glass in place, so I recommend using clear plastic or safety glass to reduce the likelihood of damage or injury or both. For a clamp to hold the glass steady, a professional grip stand works best, but you can modify a cheaper clamp. Try running a strip of heavy tape along the edges of the plastic or glass to reduce the chances that the clamp will shatter the glass or that the edge will lead to injury. Got all that? Cool.

The most common type of glass effect involves using reflections to create memorable images (Figure 47.1), including double exposures, ghost effects, and split images that form a single face from two actors. All of these involve playing with angles, like the mirror shots you mastered earlier, so be prepared to swing your camera around until the effect is complete (Figure 47.2). You may also need to make use of two separately controlled light sources.

To capture these effects, you will want to shoot through the pane of glass, framed on one of your subjects. The second subject needs to be positioned *outside* the frame, so that it can be reflected into the shot by the glass. This is where the two light sources are key, as you will light one subject traditionally and the second, reflected subject at a different intensity. The combination should cause the second subject to appear in the same shot as your main actor. Exposing two heads in one shot creates the feeling that the main character is remembering or thinking about the second "off-screen" subject.

Light the reflected subject in deep blue or green and you've got an easy ghost effect. The reflected face will obviously be slightly less in focus (or completely blurry, depending on the distance from the glass), which can add to the supernatural look of this effect. Again, you should play with angles, distances, and with varying intensities and angles of the light to see the maximum range of this trick and to achieve a look that you like. The most extreme of these works when you light each actor from a hard, side angle, and then "combine" the two lit halves of each face to form one. Running either light through a proper dimmer (check the voltage and wattage!) can allow you to "cross-fade" between these two faces or to see your "ghost" magically fade in and out of view.

Figure 47.1

Figure 47.2

TIP 48
BACKGROUND TO BASICS

Figure 48.1

Before all this digital green-screen fanciness took over, Hollywood depended on the use of giant matte paintings to relieve the burden of expensive location shoots (Figure 48.1). Instead of shipping the crew to Transylvania for a shot of Dracula's castle, studios paid an artist to paint a giant version, and then shot the actors against this massive backdrop, all without leaving Los Angeles. Now you can capture this same effect without leaving your house.

You'll need to set up your pane of glass once again. Only this time, find an interesting picture or image that you can tape to the front. My favorite is a shot of Easter Island that I clipped from a magazine — obviously a location I can't afford to fly to for a shoot. By carefully clipping out the photo, I left the foreground and some of those giant heads in the image. Once taped to my pane of glass, I can repeat the same effect that you mastered with your "Jolly Giants": forcing the perspective in the shot. Put your actor(s) several feet behind the glass, and you trick viewers into thinking that they are walking along a hill on Easter Island. The figure(s) should look small and distant as they walk along the hillside. Again, it will take you a minute to adjust so that you get the perspective right. But trust me — it's worth it.

Flipping this idea is a little tough. It isn't as easy to place small figures in the foreground with massive and impressive backgrounds behind them. But by combining a simple green-screen shot of the actor(s) with a background image, you should be able to make it work. My students pulled this off once, sending a student to the North Pole. Our actress dressed up as an elf, kneeled in front of the green screen (in an altered medium shot), and the trick rocked. Another tip involves shooting your matte with a similar background behind the pane. For example, if your matte image is a dense, tree-filled forest, take your glass pane setup to the park, and include real trees in the deep background. This will increase the illusion that your subject is truly at this location, especially if you use your focus control to complete the effect.

One last idea with this trick involves cutting out portions of a complete image. For example, you could find or make an image of a haunted castle and clip out one of the windows. By taping this to your pane of glass and placing the actors some distance behind the setup, you should be able to fool the eye into believing that they are in the castle, looking out of the window. A little creative lighting (try creating your fireplace glow here) should be the icing on the cake.

TIP 49
FLOATING FISH ATTACK

I used to scare the snot out of my video students by attacking them with the floating head of Kevin Federline, cigarette in mouth, stubble and all. Okay, not really attacking them, but I was using another awesome glass effect that is simple, fun, and effective. As before, you'll need to use some caution to avoid breaking anything, but you'll have lots of fun and are only limited by your own twisted imagination. Here's how it works.

Find a memorable image from a magazine, a photo, or a piece of art. Carefully clip it out, isolating the image (Figure 49.1). This can be a few fish, the head of a celebrity, a can of soup, whatever: The key is to clip out an object which you will tape to your clear plastic pane. You're essentially shooting for the reverse of the matte effect, isolating a single object in your image as opposed to placing a subject against a background.

By framing up a shot that incorporates a large portion of your clear pane, you should be able to create the illusion that your object is floating in the same space as your subject. By gently shaking the pane (or even the camera), you can create the effect that this otherwise static element has some life to it. You can make it appear that the school of floating fish that you clipped out is descending with a vengeance on your actor, or that a rocket ship is lifting off from a launch pad, or that the detached head of Kevin Federline is terrorizing a room full of students.

Figure 49.1

Figure 49.2

As with all glass work, take care not to include any camera reflections or glare from the lighting in your shot. This can be tricky and may take a few extra minutes to prepare (Figure 49.2), but it will help you maintain the sense of wonderment and illusion in your audience. Be sure not to let the edge of the glass or plastic show in the shot, and keep some glass cleaner around to remove streaks and smears.

TEN BY TEN, FOOLING THE EYE

THE EYES, AS THEY SAY, HAVE IT, EXCEPT WHEN YOU CAN FOOL THEM. TRY EACH OF THESE EFFECTS SHOTS, FOCUSING ON CREATING A CONVINCING ILLUSION FOR EACH EXERCISE.

1. Lock off your camera and pop some basic jump cuts of one person in one room. Have the subject find as many spots to sit or stand as possible in a single framing.

2. Head to the bathroom. Pop three mirror shots, using different shots, framings, and angles. Make someone brushing their teeth look interesting.

3. Create a campfire in your living room! Hint: Use lights, NOT REAL FIRE!

4. Using the matte painting trick, clip out some pictures of trees and set up a shot that places an actor in a dense forest. Try to master this one *indoors*.

5. Keeping your forest intact, add a pan of water and reflect a little light on your subject(s) to create the illusion that they have found a pond in the same forest.

6. Get big! Grab two friends and try setting up the "giants" forced-perspective shot. You'll know it when it lines up correctly. Then try adding two props to the illusion, one huge and one tiny. Be sure not to cross the center of the frame.

7. Create the effect of a ghost floating through your kitchen. Hint: glass pane!

8. Clip out an image of an average, ordinary row of houses. Tape it to a pane of glass and have your actor simulate a monster attacking this innocent town!

9. Find a cool picture of the moon, the *surface* of the moon. Now, using your glasswork skills, have a friend spend some time "walking" on the "moon" (playing the song by The Police is optional, but encouraged).

10. Okay, Spielberg: time to get serious. Try combining these tips to create a shot in which an actor looks into a bathroom mirror, which glows from a raging fire and is reflecting a creepy ghost. If you run out of room in the bathroom, use any mirror: in your hallway, living room, the lounge of your school, at your office, your dentist, or your church (well, maybe this isn't a good one for your church!)

SECTION 5

INTERMEDIATE ▶

50 BUTTON MASHING

There are two distinct types of errors that I see with amateur video gurus, errors that turn aspiring filmmaking geniuses into mere mortals. I call these two types of shooters "button mashers" and "flip-floppers" and I don't want you to join either group.

Button mashers rush to hit record too quickly, both to start and end a shot (or scene). Maybe it's the stress or the excitement of shooting, but in either case this can prove disastrous. There's no need to rush. Get in the habit of checking and rechecking the shot, action, or camera move and rehearsing several times, if needed, before rolling. Once you are ready, get in the habit of calling out "Rolling!" as the camera starts to record, then pausing a second before calling "Action!" It's easy to edit out the additional frames later. And it's impossible to recreate those precious few frames once shooting is over.

On the other hand, always let the camera roll a few seconds longer after you hear (or call) "Cut." Again, this is just a precaution. It's always better to have too much footage than not enough. Get in the habit of taking that extra breath, letting that extra moment pass, before cutting. You'll never have those actors in that location again, so let even the slightest moment play out and avoid hitting that button too quickly.

As for the flip-floppers, I should confess that this mistake has happened to me on a few occasions. It involves getting so caught up in the moment, in the pure thrill of shooting, that you actually end up flip-flopping, hitting "Stop" when you are supposed to roll and hitting "Record" when you need to cut. The result, of course, is pure agony, as you end up with all the in-between stuff and none of the actual scenes. This can lead to some hilarious footage and outtakes, but it also tends to mean that you have no actual shots to make into a film. It is also a surefire way to drain your batteries, collect hours of footage from inside your camera bag, and generally destroy any trust that you have developed with your cast and crew.

So take a minute to double-check that you aren't button mashing or flip-flopping. With smaller cameras (and record buttons that are easy to hit) and friends (rather than pros) helping out, both of these paths to ruin are easily discovered. The joy of shooting can distract you from either mistake. Double- and triple-check the camera each chance that you get. And save the hilarious between-takes footage for a *second* camera operator!

TIP 51
SOME IS GOOD, MORE IS BETTER

A cinematographer pal of mine from the Discovery Channel once taught me a crucial lesson: Always plan like a shooter, shoot like an editor, and edit like a writer. Huh? Just focus on the "shooting like an editor" aspect of this wisdom and it will yield generous results as you shoot (and edit) your videos.

As I mentioned when I discussed button mashing, shooting to edit involves rolling more footage than you think you need. This helps the editor build transitions, merge clips, and tell a good story. It helps both from an artistic and a technical perspective. But it involves a little more than just dodging the button-mashing demon.

Shooting to edit also involves thinking about your shots as a series of events. You need to get in the habit of both "covering" a scene, which is shooting enough footage to give the editor every possible angle and framing, and to provide options that you (or the writer, the director, and the producer) didn't see during production. This means shooting the basic stuff first, saving the complicated shots for the end of the sequence, so the editor always has a selection of shots to get through the scene. But it also means that you roll past "cut" on every shot. A common mistake with

video is that most people think that an effect, like a cross-fade, is placed onto the footage as an added element. But in digital video, effects are actually instructions for how to render, or present, the shots. Fades and other effects use portions of a clip that you may not have originally intended to be seen. In other words, the computer uses additional frames from a clip to complete the effect. By rolling each shot longer than might feel "natural," you are actually giving your editor more freedom and more information to work from in postproduction.

Finally, try to schedule your shoots to allow for time to pop a few unusual, unplanned, or unexpected shots. You may see something in the lighting, the performance, or the location that you weren't expecting. Or you may just crank out a few shots that you can give to the editor as more raw material to work from (see Tip 54 for more on this). If you keep these tips in mind, you'll start shooting for the edit and you might just stumble upon a brilliant solution along the way, even if you don't know it at the time.

TIP 52
LOCATION, LOCATION, (FAKING) LOCATIONS

Here's a big secret about TV and film, especially prime-time TV dramas and sitcoms: What you see isn't always what you get. More specifically, the exteriors of buildings that you see at the beginning of some scenes often have absolutely nothing to do with the interior(s) that you see moments later, as part of the same scene. Here's what I mean, and here's how you can use this trick to spice up your videos.

Location work for big-time TV and film is exhaustive. Skilled people build entire careers by scouting locations, dealing with building managers, snapping pre-production pictures, and discovering memorable (and workable) locations. But things don't always work out so smoothly. Shooting on location can be expensive, difficult to manage, and full of complications. Sitcoms provide a great example of this, as they depend so heavily on a common interior environment. Those familiar living rooms and kitchens you know from your favorite TV families are built on sound stages, where every aspect of production (lighting, audio, camera moves) can be carefully controlled and where an audience can see the show. But the TV audience still needs to understand where a show is taking place, the time of day, and the time period.

Enter: the establishing shot. This is a simple wide shot, or sometimes a quick tilt, of the exterior of the building or house where the story takes place. This shot establishes when and where things are happening. Watch any old episode of *Cheers* to see what I mean: The show takes place in the bar, but almost every segment opens with an exterior shot. So how can this help with *your* videos?

Let's say you're going to shoot a drama that takes place in an office. And let's say that a friend of a friend works in an actual office, and they secure permission for you to shoot there on a Saturday afternoon. Great! Except for one thing: The outside of this place not only looks terrible, but it's covered in signs for a donut shop, a dentist, and a liquor store — and none of the owners of these businesses have given you the go-ahead to shoot their (hideous) signs. No problem.

You just need to find another (more appealing) building that looks like it could be an office and get permission to shoot an establishing shot. Bingo (Figure 52.1)! Match this up with your interior footage, taking care to match any outdoor lighting conditions (especially if the interior shots reveal windows). This could be another office tower, the architecture building at your school, or even a nearby hospital, assuming you frame out the emergency entrance. I know shooters who spend "off" days popping exteriors and establishing shots, building a library of shots that they can use at any time on any project. This is an excellent idea for you to pursue, both to build up your own catalogue of shots and to keep you practicing basic wide shots. Good luck and good hunting!

Figure 52.1

53
BY A NOSE

Your next challenge is simpler than many of the other techniques in this book, but it's madly important, effective in any genre, and will dictate how you frame the majority of your shots from here on out. In the business, this type of framing is called "leading looks" or sometimes "leading space" and is a surefire way to improve your compositions and avoid another mistake that is all too common in amateur videos.

You must allow for an adequate amount of space near the top of your frame, an aspect called "headroom," so you don't cut off any heads. You also need to avoid leaving *too much* headroom, as your subjects then appear to be strangely small or they seem to float oddly below the top of the frame (Figures 53.1–2).

You must also ensure that you leave space on one side of the frame. Leading space is defined by the far edge of the frame, as dictated by the position of your subjects and either their eye line or their movement. Actors on the right side of the frame, *looking* to the left, should be framed to the right side. This gives their face some "leading room": the actor isn't oddly confined by the frame or confronted by the edge in an unappealing way. Similarly, actors *moving* to the left, regardless of the framing (wide, medium, close), should be framed to the right, giving them "leading space": space in the frame *to move into* as they progress.

Figure 53.1

Figure 53.2

In either case, with a static or a moving subject, audiences expect to see some space "in front of" the subject. Sometimes called "nose room" (so as not to chop off the end of an actor's nose), this is a comforting composition for viewers and helps you avoid some unwanted and unintended results of bad framing. Think of an actor walking to the right, but framed way too close to the right edge of the frame. Can you picture it (Figure 53.3)? It will appear that the actor is actually "dragging" the frame as she walks, a surefire path to unexpected laughter. Similarly, a static actor locked up against the left edge of the frame who is also looking to the left will appear subconsciously trapped by the frame, unable to "see" past the edge. In either case, you will (overtly or not) bring unwanted attention to the frame itself, cheapening the look of your video.

Always look at your framings, especially those that include camera moves, with the edge in mind. Make sure to "lead" your actors as they head across the frame, giving them plenty of visual space to move into. You'll want to keep your movements timed to match theirs, creating a gentle and (hopefully) unnoticed amount of comfortable space for them to move towards. And keep that frame away from noses, leaving actors some leading space to "look" into (Figure 53.4). Audiences the world over will thank you.

Figure 53.3

Figure 53.4

TIP 54
KEYS TO THE KINGDOM

A few years ago, I worked as the assistant director on an indie film shot by a rising director and an experienced director of photography (DP). We had four days to shoot a twenty-minute film on a tight budget. We shot first at an L.A. hotel and later at a for-sale house in Venice, California. The art department had made magic, converting an empty shell into the frumpy, cluttered home of an older (possibly insane?) woman in the story.

On the last day, with time running out and several shots left on the schedule, the director was frantically trying to make a decision about which shots he felt were most crucial to get in the can. I was shocked to find the DP popping random shots of the art direction, props, and scenery. Normally, as an AD, I might find this to be a bad use of time and activity, falling outside the director's vision for his film. But before I launched into an unfounded rant directed at the DP and her crew, she explained a simple but profound idea: Always get as much footage as you can, whenever you can.

Months later, when I saw the finished edit, a number of these seemingly random shots were merged into a lovely montage sequence that spoke volumes about the emotional states of the characters at that moment in the film. These were shots that weren't in the script, the storyboards, or on the precious shot list that ADs fight to complete for their directors. But they truly made that moment in the film not only possible, but memorable and effective.

Like insert shots, which you explored briefly before, cutaways can serve a number of valuable purposes. In addition to helping to tell the story, like an insert shot of a key sliding into a door handle (Figure 54.1), cutaways help to fix unplanned issues that you might run across in editing. These might include two shots that don't match (an actor with a hat on against a second shot of that actor without the hat), shots where eye lines don't match or any situation where you need a little extra something to bandage the edit. In short, you can never have too much footage, and you never know where you might use a short clip.

I used this idea on shoots that I produced for HGTV, working with my shooter to grab every possible angle, action, and coverage of both simple and complex products, people, and activities. I never met the amazing editors working for those shows (they were based in D.C.), but the feedback I got was almost always the same: not bad, just give us more. The same is now true for your videos: When shooting, always be shooting. Get your basic stuff first, tackle the toughest stuff next, and get as much cutaway footage in between. Trust me — you'll find a way to use it down the road.

Figure 54.1

TEN BY TEN, MORE IS ALWAYS BETTER

TRY EACH OF THESE QUICK EXERCISES TO FURTHER SHARPEN YOUR SHOOTING SKILLS.

1. Frame up a few of your friends in MCUs (medium close-ups), and have them do their favorite celebrity impersonation. It doesn't matter how good the performance is: The point is to make sure to leave proper headroom and nose room (leading looks).

2. Shoot a wide shot of a friend walking across your kitchen, but practice calling "Roll camera," "Action," and "Cut." Time your button mashing accordingly.

3. Repeat this same action in a tighter framing. This time, include a pan across the kitchen as your pal moves in the frame. Practice providing plenty of leading space to fit the pace of the friend's movement.

4. Now pop a quick insert into this epic kitchen video. It should be something simple, like your friend turning off the coffee pot or grabbing some keys. Make sure the action in the wider shots matches the insert.

5. Take a walk! (And bring your camera.) Practice some simple pans that include covering simple action: people walking dogs, busses rolling by, activity at a construction site. Make sure to allow for proper leading space and leading looks in each shot. Be sure to review your shots later to see how they look.

6. While you are out, see if you can grab a few random exteriors to use later as establishing shots. Remember to avoid including any signs that might define what the building actually is, and avoid shooting buildings that might, um, get you arrested, like courthouses, hospitals, and police stations.

7. Find the most cluttered room in your house and shoot cutaways of every interesting object in the room. Include a variety of framings and angles.

8, 9, and 10. It's time to combine forces. Create a short scene involving two actors talking in a familiar interior location (a living room, classroom, dorm, or office). Shoot an exterior of a *different* building. Combine this with a few shots of the two actors, starting wide and moving to tighter framings. Be sure to include at least one pan or move in your scene, complete with proper leading looks and leading room. Finish it off with a few choice cutaways or inserts (Figures 54.2–3).

Figure 54.2

Figure 54.3

≡55
THE DAY

The next three tips work like extended exercises and are three of my favorite activities for my advanced video students. Now it's your turn to try them out. But first, for these three endeavors, here are the ground rules:

1. Each exercise cannot be longer than one minute.

2. Each exercise should use exactly ten shots.

3. Each exercise can be completed in-camera (no postproduction) or edited slightly to trim the fat, selecting just the best shots for each crusade.

The first challenge is called "The Day" and involves capturing an entire day in your life. Sounds simple, yeah? Yeah, except you need to compress the whole day into ten shots, lasting only one minute. Plan accordingly. Think before you shoot. Make a list of shots that will be useful or relevant, and then be prepared to adjust as the day moves along.

The concept behind this exercise is that a total stranger could watch this snippet and get a strong sense of who you are and what you do. This type of storytelling takes some planning, some patience, and some tough decision making. Remember that each shot needs to convey significant information in a short amount of time, so focus on those moments that mean the most in your ideal day. If you want, use a friend or an actor as the subject and concentrate on directing. The point is to train your brain to capture and convey a lot of visual information in a short span of time. This will serve you well if you end up working in broadcast journalism, sports, news, advertising, or documentary film.

56 THE JOURNEY

Again, using the same three rules, your next assignment is to document "the journey." This can be any form of trip, be it the brief shuffle from your bed to the shower in the morning or an extended flight from Anchorage to Orlando. The key, once again, is to hit the high points, those critical moments that take the viewer with you, while (hopefully) sparing them the grueling, insufferable moments of boredom found on almost any trip.

Here's another way to think about this one. When my video students tackle this assignment, they always end up wedging the camera in the front windshield before driving for forty-five minutes to see their cousins. Seriously, you have no idea. Just remember that actions on-screen generally feel as if they take longer, for the viewer, than those same actions feel in real time. So spare us! We don't need to see every single moment of any given trip, even if it's just a trip across campus to the dining hall.

Less, as it turns out, really is more. There is always something that can be left aside, and ninety-nine times out of one hundred the audience will fill in the gaps. This is why characters in movies are shown getting on or off a train (plane, car, truck, scooter) and rarely during the actual trip: because the actual trip is usually mind-numbingly dull. So get to the good stuff, and shoot it well. And you don't necessarily have to think big. The best submission I have received in the years I have given this assignment showed a student of mine walking out of his apartment, to the elevator, down to his mailbox, and back again. It was short, sweet, shot well, and truly enjoyable. Remember this, and happy trails!

57 THE STORY

This one is a little trickier, but must abide by the same three rules. It's trickier because telling a significant story can mean many different things to many people. That's also what makes it so much fun. The main thing to remember: This one is all about taking your audience from the first step to the last step of a sequence. Think of any memorable series of events (try to avoid dialogue) and how best to portray them. Then start shooting.

The events, of course, need to add up to a complete story. They can range from something you can shoot in your kitchen (making a pizza is a type of story, and it tastes better than most), to something you can shoot in your neighborhood (a holiday parade or basketball tournament). The story is up to you. The hard part is finding out which moments you absolutely need, so the entire tale unfolds in one minute, and deciding *what types of shots* will best capture this epic. (Remember: You only get ten.)

Once again, a little planning is in order. Let's look at the pizza example in more detail. Have you ever watched those daytime talk shows, where the host meets up with a fancy chef to demonstrate an insane recipe that you can (supposedly) master at home? They always have the basic ingredients and foods and then a more complete version of the dish that's almost ready to eat? Why? Because TV can't wait forty-five minutes while the thing actually bakes in the oven. You have the same challenge with this exercise: finding a way to capture all the steps for the viewer, while cutting nonessential elements in "the story." Good luck. And save a slice of pizza for me.

TIP 58
BACK AND FORTH

Here's a shooting method for covering a basic scene with two characters that is popular, useful, and easy to execute. Known as the shot/reverse shot technique, this approach has been used for ages in films, dramas, talk shows, news magazine shows, and comedies.

For this exercise, plan to shoot a simple game of cards between two friends. This can be in your dorm room, living room, a coffee shop — almost any location. There is no need for dialogue or any elaborate staging, since you should keep the focus exclusively on the shots you need. And here's the really good news: For basic shot/reverse shot coverage, you really only need three shots to get through the scene.

You'll want to start with a reasonable wide or medium wide shot that shows both actors and enough of the location or background so the audience understands where the scene is taking place (Figure 58.1). Determine a significant starting and ending point for the scene, as you will need to repeat the sequence in the other two shots. And this is the key to making this coverage work: being able to repeat simple actions in different framings. Run the scene a few times, rolling your wide or medium wide shot.

Figure 58.1

Once you have this "master" shot in the can, pick the actor on the right side, reframe to set him or her up in a medium or MCU, and repeat the scene, shooting this angle. Naturally, you will want to match the action as closely as possible to the wide shot. Once you have this angle covered, reframe to cover the actor on the left in a similar framing, and repeat the sequence once more (Figures 58.2–3). If you maintained the action and the sequence, you should now have three shots that can be cut together in almost any order during editing, allowing you a number of choices for working through the scene.

Here are a few important tips to keep in mind. Make sure to give the actor on the right some leading space to the left, and vice versa, using your rule of thirds to place the actors to the same side of the screen where they are physically positioned. This helps the audience to follow the action and avoids a situation in which elements "jump" unexpectedly from one side of the screen to the other. This is known as "continuity of the frame" and helps audiences keep their (visual) bearings. Look for interesting points in the action to cut from one framing to the next, such as a card being picked up or placed down on a table, a change in eye line (from near to far or from the left-hand character to the cards that the right-hand character is holding). And once you have this basic technique down solid, try adding in a few more framings (close-ups and inserts) to bring out the full potential for the scene (see next tip for more info).

Figure 58.2

Figure 58.3

59 IN THE CAN

The basic shot/reverse shot method will get you through any simple sequence, especially with two actors and simple actions. For a more elaborate approach or for scenes with more characters, more action, or more elements to cover, you'll need a more complex plan of attack. Since the variety of combinations is almost limitless, the basic strategy to follow involves working from wide to tight shots when covering the scene.

As before, the smartest method is to cover the entire scene, from start to finish, with a static master, usually a wide or medium wide, showing the entire cast and their environment. This is also sometimes referred to as a "safety," since it captures all the necessary ingredients in one simple shot. The only problem, of course, is that it can be terribly boring to look at one scene from one wide angle for very long. But grab a master anyway, just to be sure. You can also refer back to this master by playing back the footage if you need to match a certain action, line of dialogue, or placement of an actor, prop, or piece of scenery.

Once your master is in the can (shot to your satisfaction, with all technical concerns addressed), move to tighter and tighter framings. Pick a medium for one actor, frame it up, and run the scene again. Then move in for a medium close-up or close-up *on the same actor*, from roughly the same angle. This

helps more experienced actors give you increasingly significant performances (trust me — they know when the camera is pointed their way). This also cuts down on the number of times you need to move the camera and adjust lighting. Next, repeat this process for a second actor and even a third. Once you have the principal actors "shot out," you can move toward grabbing any extreme close-ups, inserts, or crucial cutaways for that scene. An example might be an actor reaching for a certain prop (a weapon, a cell phone) that the other characters cannot see.

Only when all of this is in the can should you try any complicated camera moves or artsy shots. Finish the cake before putting on the frosting, if you get what I mean. For more advanced coverage, like dolly shots with a moving actor, I would work the same way: Start with a (moving) master and then cut in for closer coverage. The only time I would break from this method is when a director is convinced that a more cinematic approach is appropriate and sufficient. An example might be a character racing through a crowd, shot entirely with a handheld camera, or a single character pondering his fate on a solitary park bench, shot in an extreme wide shot, with no cuts. As your skills grow, you can go for more complicated opening shots, but you should still treat them as a master.

TIP 60
THIS WAY OUT

Another classic trap that most amateurs fall into involves scenes or shots that cut when a subject is still moving across the frame or is attempting an entrance or exit. By focusing on not being a button masher and rolling before calling "Action" (and after calling "Cut"), you can avoid most of these issues. To further avoid bad cuts, you will need to practice shooting clean "E and Es" (shorthand for entrances and exits).

This is really an exercise in patience and focus. On one level, grabbing clean E and Es simply means letting your actors move entirely through a course of action while the camera is rolling (Figures 60.1–5). For example, you set up a shot of an actor walking through a door. Simple, right? But you would be surprised at how many times new filmmakers cut while their actor is *almost* through the door or when the door has *almost* closed. Leave those razor sharp decisions for the editing process. Let the entire entrance or exit run to its completion while rolling, even if it feels like you should cut. Worse yet, you often see bad edits made because the shooter cut while the actor was halfway in or out of the frame, causing an awkward visual leap for your audience or an unexpected jump that makes it look like your actor has magically teleported out of the scene.

On a deeper level, clean E and Es also involve allowing on-screen actions to be completed without cutting. Take the card game example that you shot earlier. Let's say the character on the right needs to draw two cards to complete a hand. In the master and in the coverage shots, have this actor complete the range of action *entirely* without cutting. With a bit of luck and rehearsal, the same action will be intact in both shots, giving you every opportunity to make a clean cut from one shot to the next during the edit. A common phrase used in production and by editors is "cutting on the action." This means that even the simplest cut looks cleaner when you make the edit exactly as a particular action occurs. This not only "hides" the cut, but the audience is more forgiving of edits between framings or angles, as the action carries them through the edit. This is always a good goal for completing edits and is almost impossible to achieve without shooting clean E and Es.

Stay focused, resist the temptation to button mash, and let the action play out entirely. This continuity of action depends on the actors, of course, but the director shares responsibility for getting it right. From entrances and exits to simple movements like picking up a coffee cup or taking off a hat, let it roll, baby. And keep it clean.

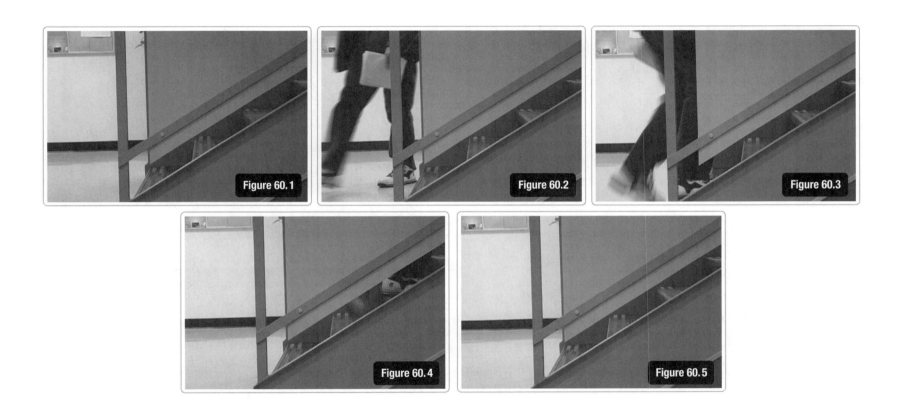

Figure 60.1

Figure 60.2

Figure 60.3

Figure 60.4

Figure 60.5

61 GOING DUTCH

A fun and relatively easy-to-shoot option for certain scenes or videos involves cranking your horizon line off kilter. Known as "Dutch angles," these shots bring an unreal, psychedelic, bizarre, or psychologically disturbing quality to your visual storytelling palette. Favored by such filmmakers as Terry Gilliam, "Dutching" tips the scales towards the surreal, grabs your audience without completely disorienting them, and opens up the more cinematic aspects of your stories (Figures 61.1–2). Best used for music videos, certain moments in sporting events, psychological thrillers, and some comedies, Dutching will bring an exciting, dynamic element to your videos.

Fair warning: Most basic tripods actually make it difficult to execute Dutch angles easily. These beginner sets of sticks are made to help you shoot correctly with the horizon nice and even. To get beyond this, you can spend a bazillion bucks renting or buying an advanced tripod, one that adds more options with additional controls that allow you to alter the shooting angle with a high degree of precision. But there are several options to capture this memorable type of shot, all of which you can pull off easily.

Figure 61.1

Figure 61.2

The easiest way to Dutch, but the one that involves the *least* amount of control, is to shoot handheld with your hand cocked to one side or the other. This can work well, but keep in mind that you don't want to tip the frame too drastically or you will end up with what I call "Titanic Syndrome": where your horizon is so grossly angled that it looks like your subjects are on a sinking ship. Keeping the horizon under a twenty-five-degree angle will help you avoid this problem (Figure 61.3).

Figure 61.3

Another approach to grabbing Dutch angles is to rotate the camera on the tripod plate slightly so that when you tilt the tripod head, you are actually changing the angle of the shot; thus, the horizon rotates from the left or right instead of moving up and down as it would with a traditional tilt. Certain tripod heads allow for this fairly easily; others may not. Likewise, certain cameras and plates have two posts

that line up in only one way, which will actually prevent you from Dutching on your tripod. You'll need to experiment to find out where you stand.

Many tripods, especially those intended for still photography, include options for Dutching. But if you still can't make it work, there's another option. Take the camera off the tripod, and place it on a sandbag, pillow, chair cushion, or rolled-up jacket or sweatshirt. This creates a solid base for the camera and opens up options. In particular, you can rotate the camera slightly on this soft base to create a range of Dutch angles for your shot. Be careful not to let a segment of the fabric inch in front of your lens, and take a moment to make sure the camera is balanced well so that it doesn't roll, flip, or fall out of place. Then you can Dutch to your heart's content, or until you start to feel sick.

TEN BY TEN, DUTCH TREATS

RUN THROUGH EACH OF THESE EXERCISES TO GET YOUR SHOTS TO SIZZLE.

1. Homework time! Don't worry: This won't hurt *too* much. All you need to do is zip through your DVDs and find five different scenes that use a typical shot/reverse shot method for covering a scene. See? I told you it wouldn't hurt.

2. Be honest. You didn't shoot the scene in which two of your friends play cards, did you? You just skimmed over that part, saying, "Oh, yeah. I got it." All right, slick, you got it. Now prove it. Shoot a three-minute card game played by two of your amigos. Which game you play is up to you, but I recommend Texas Hold 'Em.

3. No, not done yet. Cover this same game again, this time adding close-ups, two inserts, and a cutaway. Oh, and add a third character as a waiter or waitress bringing refreshments to the table. Make sure you get clean E and Es.

4. Speaking of clean E and Es, put together a sequence in which a subject moves through at least two doorways and completes another simple action, like taking off shoes, hanging up a jacket, or picking up a briefcase before exiting. Make sure each action runs completely through each framing, shot, or angle.

5. Go watch a Terry Gilliam film, any Terry Gilliam film. Then watch it again.

6. Pass the Dutchie! Make a one-minute video focusing on your car, your bike, favorite chair, or even your outdoor grill. The subject almost doesn't matter; the point is to get some Dutch angles going. Try shooting some handheld and try some more using a soft cushion to steady your camera.

7. Have a friend sit in front of your computer. Practice covering this "scene" by shooting a wide shot and then a sequence of framings that move closer and closer, ending with an extreme close-up of the friend's fingers typing on the keyboard. Now shoot a few Dutch angles of your friend. See how bizarre and disturbing you can make him or her appear (assuming, of course, that your friend isn't significantly bizarre and disturbing to begin with). Grab a handheld shot that begins with a normal angle and slowly start slipping into a Dutch angle. How does this change the story that you are telling?

8, 9, and 10. Think of a series of locations where you can shoot. Grab a friend and have her or him walk from one location to the next. You don't need to shoot every step of the way. Instead, focus on getting clean E and Es, so that each exit and each subsequent entrance almost flow together. Ideally, you should end up with a few key shots that show a single person moving through three or so locations, without all the boring steps in between. Each exit should almost match the next entrance and so on.

62 NOUNS ON THE MARCH

You've probably been taught that the idea of balance is essentially one of equality, that two plus two always equals four and that the center is always in the middle of a circle. But when you start to investigate the idea of balance from a visual perspective, most of this thinking goes out the window. Especially in a rectangular environment, visual elements carry different "weights" for the viewer, and, because of this, we need to revisit our notion of balance, centering, and composition. Here are some guidelines.

For starters, recall that the center of your image is often the weakest *visual* portion of the frame. Certain directors actually exploit this notion. Wes Anderson, for example, often presents characters positioned dead center in the middle of the frame, increasing the sense of awkwardness that comes *from* the character and is felt by the viewer.

Balance in visual compositions is also determined by such elements as shape, line, size, height, color, texture, pattern, and depth (Figure 62.1). I know, I know, that's a lot to try to digest. Here's the best way to try to comprehend the idea of visual weight and how it affects balance in your shots: Small elements with lots of visual weight will balance against larger elements with less (Figure 62.2). For

Figure 62.1

Figure 62.2

example, a character wearing a bright red scarf will "balance" (visually) against a large neutral surface, like a wall, a crowd, or an empty street. A heavily textured object, taking up little room in the frame, will balance against a larger object that has less texture. An actor in a wide shot on the left of the frame will balance against the negative space on the right (Figure 62.3).

Got it? I didn't think so. Here's what you do: Take several random items from around your house, like soda cans, action figures, juice bottles, hats, whatever. Set up your camera so you are shooting a simple environment, like a plain wall, with a surface in the foreground. Place various objects on the table top and practice balancing them, one at a time and then two at a time, within this simple framing (Figure 62.4). Roll about fifteen seconds for each composition and then look back at the footage. You should notice that certain objects, colors, or placements dominate. By making small adjustments, see how well you can achieve balance in your shots. Remember, practice makes perfect.

Figure 62.3

Figure 62.4

TIP 63
THE ZEN OF ACTOR PLACEMENT

My students always struggle with the eternal question of where to put actors in the frame, peppering me with questions as they prepare to shoot even the most basic scenes. And while there are almost limitless possibilities — depending on the scene itself, location(s), camera moves, and other factors — I have found that by exploring two simple solutions, most problems regarding actor placement easily vanish.

The first solution involves scenes with two actors, which will be a huge portion of the material you will shoot. The easiest solution involves keeping the actors on different planes, creating an angle between them, and exploiting the Z axis to increase a sense of depth in the image. In other words, avoid putting both actors in a straight line relative to each other, either horizontally across the frame or vertically, which leads to one actor mostly blocking the second. Keep several feet between the two, moving away from the lens, and aligned along the Z axis. Watch that the eye lines connect, and make sure to maintain continuity of the frame between cuts (see Tip 69).

When dealing with three actors, use triangular compositions whenever possible (Figure 63.1). The magic of the triangle enables you to increase not only the sense of depth, but also the sense of strength and balance from this natural, organic, and easy-to-execute arrangement (Figure 63.2). Check out the opening sequence from *Once Upon a Time in the West* for a crash course in the use of triangular actor placements. It's brilliant (Figures 63.3–4).

For larger scenes, consider isolating a single significant character on one side of the frame, balanced against a large group. Or place your main character in the foreground, balanced against a group positioned further from the lens. Try setting off the main character with colorful costume choices. These are examples of the backwards type of balance that we must master with visual storytelling. In the real world, balance would mean that you have five people on one side and five on the other. But visually this looks awkward and unnatural, and in most cases will give your frame an odd, forced feeling. Stick to angles, triangles, and isolated groupings and your scenes will start to sing.

Figure 63.1

Figure 63.2

Figure 63.3

Figure 63.4

ᵀᴵᴾ64 BLOCK PARTY

So you have a handle on where to put actors in a static shot. Now you have a new problem to face: how to get them moving and what to do with that boring shot. Again, there are a multitude of possible solutions, and they hinge on the nature of the scene, the limits of the locations, and the skill of the camera operator, but here are a few quick tips that will get you moving or at least get your actors moving.

First, let's cover some vocabulary words. Don't worry — they're easy, and there won't be a quiz. Blocking is the theatrical term used to describe the specific movements of actors in a scene (Figure 64.1). Crossing is another theater term, which is used to describe an actor moving from one place to another, usually horizontally, but also diagonally. Upstage is action away from the audience (or lens) and downstage is action towards the audience (or lens). More commonly, we describe action as moving frame left or frame right, as captured in our image (Figure 64.2). A simpler description for actors (no offense, actors!) is to use the terms *camera left* or *camera right* (which is the opposite of frame left and frame right). Don't tell the actors; it will just confuse them (joking, actors! Love ya!).

Figure 64.1

Figure 64.2

An obvious choice is always to move the camera along with the movement of the action or actor(s). For example, a character walking down a street can be covered nicely with a shot that tracks or pans in the same direction (Figure 64.3). An actor climbing a set of stairs or a ladder is a good place to tilt. Moving the camera in the opposite direction can be tricky, but interesting. Consider a pan to the left to reveal a seated actor who then rises and crosses to the right.

For static shots, have your actors move diagonally, exploiting the Z axis as much as possible. With two actors, try having them cross in opposite directions, again along a diagonal path. In group situations (Figure 64.4), you can create powerful images by simply having your actor move against the tide, or by *not* moving as the world swirls past him or her. In general, stick to broad directions and leave the small stuff to the performer. For instance, give them a starting point and a stopping point and perhaps suggest a pace, but let them decide when to remove a hat, adjust their tie, or perform any other small business.

Think organically and think suggestively. In other words, use basic shapes and patterns (circles work well), as well as exploring variations in visual weight and balance. But also consider what the movement itself can express; an actor struggling to walk against a sea of bodies on a New York City street at rush hour might suggest some interesting themes. For more complicated blocking or when you want an actor to stop, turn, or speak at a certain spot, mark the ground with a small strip of tape. Take a moment for a brief rehearsal before shooting scenes with more complex blocking.

Figure 64.3

Figure 64.4

65 MATCH GAME

Another common trick used extensively in film and TV is called the match cut, and, with a touch of planning, it's easy to shoot. With a little creative thinking, a match cut can also prove memorable for your viewers. Here's how it works.

In simple terms, match cuts are used by editors to avoid jump cuts. Jumps, as you know, involve showing the viewer an unexpected leap in time or space. Match cuts work in the opposite manner, joining two seemingly different shots by cutting just as the two shots share a common element. Picture an actor hanging up a phone. In one shot, we see a character finishing a phone call. Her hand extends downward to hang up the receiver. In the next shot, we see a telephone receiver landing in its place but then tilt up to reveal another character just finishing a phone call. This can either imply that the two characters were speaking to each other, or it can simply serve as an interesting and unexpected visual bridge between scenes or shots.

Known sometimes as "cutting on a common object," match cuts that share a similar object or action are used universally to join scenes together. For example, a character about to exit through a doorway is cut to match a different character entering through a similarly framed door. Match cuts are also common in montage sequences. Picture a typical city-dwelling character in a romantic comedy on a shopping spree in Manhattan. You tend to see her in a rapid-fire burst of similar shots, ringing out purchases at a number of different cash registers, for example. Match cuts can also be dramatic. Picture a character in a thriller with a sealed manila envelope who may then be shown hiding that envelope in a safe place. But if you match cut to the next scene, showing the envelope placed on the desk of the villain in the story, you've increased the tension and the drama. How did it get there? Is the main character safe or in trouble? Will the villain open the envelope?

Match cuts can also help advance the story. Hitchcock's match cut at the end of *North by Northwest* is a well-documented example of this version of the trick. And his cutting to common shapes during the shower scene in *Psycho* was so effective that it still resonates across the cinematic landscape. You might find similar uses, or use it simply as an interesting method for linking two distinct but related moments in your video.

The key is to decide exactly which objects, colors, shapes, or movements you want to match, find a place in your story where this effect will make sense or strengthen your message, and then plan, practice, and pop the shot. The possibilities artistically, stylistically, and thematically are almost limitless. So pick your shots, tell your editor, and start matching.

TIP 66
END GAME

I touched briefly on the idea of start frames and end frames — elements within a shot that help to define where a camera move begins and ends — and the time has come to explore this idea a bit further. From the simplest tilt or pan to more advanced dolly moves, whip pans, or handheld shots, start and end frames help your cast and crew understand exactly how, when, and where you expect a shot to begin and terminate. And, if you plan well and rehearse once or twice, you might even make a little art. Here goes.

When you first attack a project and create a shot list of all the crucial ways that you want to tell the story, you won't define start and end frames. You will simply scribble something quickly like "Pan from door to desk as Denise crosses with briefcase." Once you are shooting, however, everything from the focus to the lighting to the rate at which the actress playing Denise moves will be defined by start and end frames. That's the technical way of looking at this concept. A more artistic way to look at things might be to decide that the scene is really all about this mysterious briefcase, especially since at this point in the story Denise isn't certain what's *inside* the briefcase. So your start frame will be at the door, knee height, with the briefcase in focus. Denise needs to cross while keeping the case at the same height, and as she swings it up onto her desk, the camera needs to pedestal up, widen out a touch, and end with the case centered in the shot. Bingo: Start frame and end frame defined, and all the participants know what to expect. Pop a quick rehearsal or two, and then shoot the scene. (Side note: Always shoot the rehearsal!)

Pay attention to props, architecture, objects, and the details of the location for pointers on what to use as "marks" to make sure your camera crew finds their frames exactly the same way for each take. Bring a few rolls of different colored tape along to mark spots for the actors and for the camera and dolly crews. It's much easier than guessing and more accurate than saying something vague like "Just line up with the third chair from the left." If you want to get real pro, contact a film or theatrical supply store and order some "spike tape." This tape is sturdy and affordable, it doesn't damage most surfaces, you can write on it, and it comes in a variety of colors, including digital green. You can become super pro and assign specific colors (red for actors, yellow for camera, blue for audio, and so forth) for each department or for starting and ending marks (green to start and red for stopping points). But any system will work, so long as you and the crew agree. (Side note: This is not always the case, especially when it comes to when lunch is and how long lunch lasts.) Got all that? Good, now go practice.

TIP67 WORTH A THOUSAND WORDS

In 1965 Bob Dylan released one of his first electric folk songs, ripping another crack in the facade of the status quo, catapulting the Beats and their agenda to the forefront, and influencing several generations of songwriters, political protestors, dropouts, and deviants. A short promotional film for the song, "Subterranean Homesick Blues" features a young, hip Dylan displaying a series of cards directly to the camera which echo certain lyrics from the song, purposeful misspellings and all. Why should *you* care? Because the clip, originally intended to open D. A. Pennebaker's film, *Dont Look Back* (which covered Dylan's then-current tour of England), has been credited by some as the original music video, and it has been influencing video and filmmakers ever since.

Poke around YouTube for a few minutes. Check out the interpretation by INXS (*Mediate*), the truly brilliant, palindrome-fueled homage *Bob* from "Weird Al" Yankovic, and the scores of other imitations floating around out there. What do they all have in common? They have taken Dylan's transformation of words into objects as a technique for visual storytelling and run with it, and now it's your turn.

Obviously, you won't see much of this approach in traditional TV, like news or sports. But for your next music video, political rant, art flick, or even your next school project, you can either recreate a version of Dylan's single-shot masterpiece (complete with tacky but effective zoom in the beginning) or create a variation all your own. The point is that directly confronting the audience by changing mere words into powerful visual elements, whether they appear on simple white cards or not, is a compelling method of communication.

Avoid falling into the trap of simply adding type or graphics to your clips. There is simply something incredibly captivating about a subject holding the words, tossing them around, and forcing them to the forefront of your viewers' attention before discarding them — an effect that is impossible with digitally generated graphics. You should also be wary of prefabricated graphics in certain software.

So grab some cards, some markers, and a message and get busy. I personally recommend those smelly markers from elementary school. You know, the ones that smell like blueberries and oranges and stuff? Just remember to clean up the signs after you throw each one on the ground.

TIP 68
CAMERA IN A COAL MINE

As I hinted before, a big drawback to the trend in cameras becoming smaller and smaller is that they are harder to control with precision when it comes to complex camera moves, especially those that are handheld. But the flip side, the positive part of the drop in camera size, is that you can stick them almost anywhere you need to get the shot.

A few years back, a director buddy of mine showed me a crime drama he shot using a 16mm film camera. In the piece, he managed to stuff the camera in his fridge to pop a shot of a criminal hiding some loot next to the cold cuts and ketchup (Figure 68.1). This might not seem like a big deal, but at the time, with a big camera and no remote control, this was a fairly difficult shot to execute. The advantage is that you can stick your high-end HD camcorder in just about any small space and produce memorable shots that will spice up your videos for no extra cost.

The key, of course, is not to overdo it: You'll want to find just the right moment in your project to give your audience that unique perspective. Aside from that concern, you can easily shove your camera in a mailbox, stove, shoebox, trunk of a car, glove compartment, desk drawer, kitchen cupboard, closet… almost any tight place that can be opened or closed and makes sense in the context of the story.

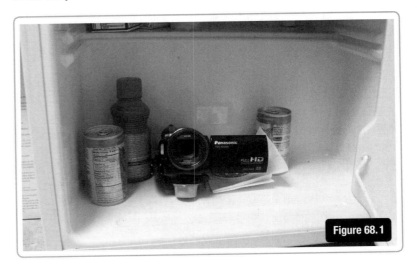

Figure 68.1

Here are a couple of quick pointers. Obviously, these types of shots work best once edited. First, you'll need to start rolling, close the door or lid or cabinet, play the scene (which ideally involves opening and then closing the door, lid, or whatever), and then open things up again to hit stop. You'll need to remember to trim all that extra footage away later. Second, be prepared to include a sweatshirt, small pillow, or a sandbag on which to balance the camera; the last thing you want to happen is your camera to accidentally roll over into the potato salad when the door to the fridge closes. Third, try using your remote to stop and start the roll, saving you all that extra footage to chop out later. This may not work through a fridge door, but it might be possible through a thin surface or in a situation where you have a line of sight to the camera (like via a second kitchen cupboard door). Last, you can use two of these in a row to set up a knockout transition between scenes. For example, your character places a significant prop in an interesting place, like a car trunk (Figure 68.2). Bang! The trunk closes, and the screen goes black. You start the next scene with the same guy in a different location opening a closet, and you've got your transition.

Examples of this type of technique abound, but I recommend checking out the shots from inside the warden's safe towards the end of *The Shawshank Redemption* (Figure 68.3): a brilliant moment for this type of shot from a storytelling perspective, masterfully executed, and memorable. The director was able to repeat this trick with devastating effect, especially for the warden. Now it's your turn. Grab your camera, find that special hiding place, and get stuffed.

Figure 68.2

Figure 68.3

TEN BY TEN, GETTING STUFFED

EXERCISE

HERE ARE TEN QUICK PRACTICE EXERCISES TO HELP YOU STUFF YOUR CAMERA INTO ALL KINDS OF MEMORABLE PLACES, FOR THE GREATER GOOD AND ADVANCEMENT OF CINEMA, OF COURSE.

1. Get the mail (assuming of course that you have a big mailbox). Stick your camera inside and reach for some bills.

2. What's the best part about Thanksgiving? Leftovers! Shove your camera in the fridge next to the olives. For an advanced version, put the camera on a serving tray and actually take it out, walking all the way to the table while rolling. Hot soup!

3. Drop your camera in a closet, then have an actor open the door to hide a bag of money, briefcase, or other suspicious item. You get bonus points for using that item to black out the lens to complete the shot.

4. Practice setting up start and end frames by having a friend complete some simple actions, such as walking down a hall through a doorway into a room, sitting at a table, or even pouring coffee. Shoot each one at least three times, and then compare the takes. Do you hit the same mark, or frame, each time?

5. Grab three friends and practice placing actors in various framings, from wide to medium. Try at least three locations, including an interior, a common public place like a lounge, bar or office, and an exterior like a park, dry cleaner, or zoo. You get bonus points at the zoo if you can also get several monkeys to form a triangular blocking pattern.

6. Set up a static wide shot and invite three friends over. Have them run through a basic scene; it can be about anything, but keep it simple. Focus on blocking the actors without moving the camera. Try various organic and natural types of movements: circles, crosses, diagonals. Repeat the scene using three different types of actor movement.

7. Match it up! Try some simple match cuts. Remember: This combines two separate shots that share a common visual element. Examples include a person finishing a phone call, an object placed on a table, or a car door closing.

8, 9, and 10. Think up a quick scenario that will allow you to combine a match cut; a camera stuffed into a box, cabinet, dresser drawer, or fridge; and a shot that involves a start and end frame. Make sure this masterpiece lasts no more than one minute. Again, bonus points if you can somehow incorporate monkeys.

SECTION 6

ADVANCED ▶

TIP 69
KEEPING IT REEL

Of the topics that my students love to explore, errors in continuity are easily the most popular. This phenomenon has been repeated all over YouTube, with scores of people chronicling the slightest errors between shots: A pen moves from one hand to the other, a drink "refills" as a scene progresses, hats jump on and off heads, and ties magically appear and disappear. And while inconsistencies with continuity of action must be addressed, an equally crucial area to pay attention to involves what is called "continuity of the frame." Simply put, this means keeping elements that first appear on the right (or left) of the frame on the right (or left) in subsequent shots. The more complex approach to this uses something called the "line of action," also known as the "180 degree line" or simply "the line." Here's what it's all about.

Picture a standard scene, set in a living room. Two actors share the space, which includes a sofa in the middle, a soft, green chair on the right, and a wooden chair on the left. The camera is first placed parallel to the sofa, framed in a wide shot. As soon as you roll, "the line" is established, an imaginary boundary parallel to the lens and running across the scene, directly through the actors. Now imagine a giant circle, cut in half by the line. From now on, no matter where you put the camera, as long as you remain within the 180 degrees to the same side of the line as you began, you won't violate this rule or disorient your audience: In short, you'll maintain continuity of the frame. You can pick any angle and any framing,

while staying on one side of the line. The actor on the right, in the green comfy chair, will always appear screen right and likewise for the actor on the left. As for any props or objects that are moved, you will need to work with your actors to ensure consistency of actions they take during the course of the scene.

Are you out of angles, or do you need to spice up the sequence? There are a few ways to cross the line without freaking out or confusing your audience. You can cross it if the camera continues to roll while it physically crosses over. You can also cross if you first place the camera on the line, to point directly at one actor from the other performer's point of view, for instance. And finally, *movement of the actors* over the line or the entrance of another performer can allow you to "jump" the line. But use caution: It takes some practice to master this approach, as a *new line* is established in each of these instances.

TIP 70
KEN BURNS CALLING

One area that isn't often explored by amateurs involves shooting video of photos (or posters or artwork, basically anything flat or printed). With the exception of documentaries, I think this is a hugely underexplored area in filmmaking, perhaps because most people think it's too difficult. But here's the truth: As long as you are willing to think backwards, it's easy.

What do I mean by thinking backwards? The solution is to move the photos, keeping the camera locked off for each shot. Think about it: Most flat images that you might shoot, whether they are historical photos, an old family album, or a map of Civil War battle lines, are probably small and a little fuzzy. To get a decent shot, you need to zoom in tight, making any camera move (panning across an image, for instance) awkward to execute. By locking off the shot and gently moving the image through the shot (to simulate your pan), you can maintain a high degree of control, keep the image in focus, and avoid any jarring camera shakes or shudders. You should also avoid anything but very basic — non-colored lighting — as you want the image to speak for itself.

You can buy an expensive rig to hang your camera over a photo. But a cheaper solution is simply to tape or tack the photo on a wall, preferably against a sheet of black poster board (Figure 70.1). This works great for larger photos or printed images, especially if you can still do a slow zoom or pan across. For smaller pictures, you may need to lay your black poster board and photo(s) on a flat surface and crank your tripod so you are almost shooting down at the image. Then lock off the shot and slowly drag or rotate the photo in an interesting way. For really delicate or small photos, simply drag the whole poster board. Just be careful not to get any shadows or camera reflections in the shots.

Figure 70.1

For more cumbersome stuff, like books, you may need to get a little creative. For example, two of my students once did a news story about the class of 1956 donating a gift to the high school. They wanted to supplement interviews they shot with footage of the actual 1956 yearbook, which they managed to find in the main office. They placed the yearbook on a desk, added a little light, and then carefully framed up the shot so that it was just tight enough to exclude one student's hand. She then gracefully opened the book to show the senior class pictures, rotating the entire yearbook slightly at the same time. It was truly a masterful, elegant solution and worked much better than two separate shots of the yearbook cover, edited next to a shot of the interior pages.

Needless to say, the story came out great, they both earned an "A," and this was without reading this book! So grab those family albums (Figure 70.2), an old year-book, or your softball team photo, snag a sheet of black poster board, and get shooting! Who knows? The next time your phone rings, it could be Ken Burns calling.

Figure 70.2

TIP71 THE PRODUCT AS HERO

Admit it: We all have heroes of the silver (and small) screen. From James Bond to Indiana Jones to Buffy, Ripley, and Trinity, we worship them, follow every daring exploit, and buy action figures that resemble them (note: I don't actually own any Buffy action figures). We're just dying to work on their next film. In the meantime, it's wise to admit that more often than not it's *the product* that's the (paying) hero.

Advertising drives huge amounts of the entertainment we consume daily. And advertising depends heavily on product shots, those moments at the end of ads that show a jar of peppers in all its glory (Figure 71.1). These shots are often called "hero" shots, and pro crews can spend hours getting a can of taco sauce to look *just right*. The good news for you? These people are paid well for their troubles. Trust me.

What does this have to do with your videos? Two things. One, I hope that your stuff will be good enough to get *you* paid eventually. And two, you may come across a moment in your own videos when you'll need to make a bottle of soda look as impressive as possible. This could be for a school project, an infomercial, a report to your coworkers, or just something for fun that you shoot with friends. The key is to be able to create an environment in which you can isolate just the product, add a dash of lighting for effect, and snag a memorable shot of that can of shaving cream.

Figure 71.1

You'll want a fresh sheet of poster board. And you'll want a few colors, namely white, black, and maybe even digital green. These don't need to be huge, but they should be free of scratches, price tags, or other distracting markings. You'll want to find a secure, flat spot in your house, dorm, or office, preferably one that meets up with a smooth wall. Mount the poster board so that about two-thirds of it is flat against the wall, and the final stretch runs down to the flat surface, curving gently just where the wall meets the surface where you will shoot. Grab a few strips of matching tape (black, white, green) and secure the edges of the poster board (Figure 71.2). Got it?

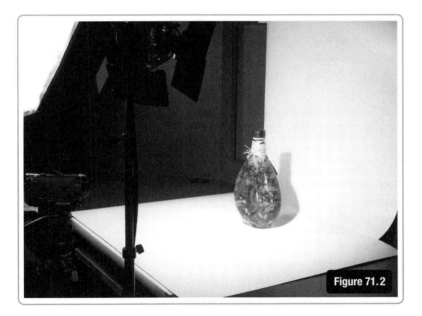

Figure 71.2

What you've just simulated is a mini-version of a cyclorama, a special curved backdrop found on professional sound stages. The point of the curve is to help fool the camera into "seeing" an endless background, without a defined corner or edge. Think about any ad (with a product or real people) in which the subject or object is isolated against an endless white world, and you'll know what I mean. This effect works best (especially against the white environment) when you slam a bunch of light into the shot and iris back down for a good exposure. The result should be a shot that puts all the attention on the product, no matter if it's an energy drink, pair of running shoes, or a solar-powered stapler.

This technique is also great for shooting clips of sculpture, figurines, plastic models, trophies, cell phones or electronics, and almost any kind of food. You won't be able to do much panning or tilting, as the effect is ruined if your viewer sees past the edge of your "set." Try using a simple plastic Lazy Susan to get the product rotating in cool ways. Chalk up more bonus points if you can dramatically dim the lighting at just the right moment. Hmmm. Olives with taco sauce? Maybe not.

TIP 72
STAYING FOCUSED. OR NOT.

Playing with focus is easily one of my favorite in-camera techniques for increasing visual interest, finding unique ways to tell stories, and exploring unexpected dynamics within an image. Snapping from an out-of-focus shot to reveal an in-focus building, sign, or character is a gripping, memorable example. Pulling out of a blur of light and pixels to expose an important object, actor, or location is another favorite. This trick works in an almost limitless number of genres: You see it in live sports, dramas, music videos, flashbacks and dream sequences, news shows, and action scenes. That's the good news.

The bad news is that many affordable camcorders actually limit the possibilities of changing focus within a single shot. This might be because of the design: The focus control might be in a difficult-to-access menu or too small to adjust focus with precision. The more advanced (and expensive) cameras work better because they often include a focus ring, a wheel-like device near the lens that you can slowly (or quickly) spin to change the focus. Whether or not you have this luxury, or if you are forced to change focus using your remote or a small toggle, be sure to explore the full range of possibilities that this trick provides.

Keep a few key points in mind when changing focus. First, you can think of almost any image (except super-tight framings) as consisting of three planes: a foreground (one to five feet from the lens), middle ground (five to twenty feet), and the background (twenty feet and beyond). Once you can "see" this consistently, the power of easily changing focus starts to emerge. For instance, picture a scene with two actors separated by several feet. If one actor is in the foreground and the second is in the background, "pulling focus" between the two (especially at key moments in the scene) is a truly effective type of storytelling. You can do this easily by ignoring the traditional method for setting focus (zooming all the way in first) and instead establish focal points for each plane separately. In other words, if you pick the foreground actor, find the spot where they are in focus and remember it (either on your focus ring, in your menu, or by trusting your eye). Do the same for the second actor in the background by setting a different focal point. Then, by subtly sliding between the two, you can force your audience to pay more attention to one actor or the other at different points in the scene.

You can also use this trick when shooting exteriors. I love to pull focus between the sign of an establishment (in the foreground) and the actual exterior of that location (in the background). This works well when combined with music or a voice over and is a great spin on using a static, traditional establishing shot. Pull-focus shots are used all the time for crowd shots, especially for news or news magazine shows and videos. How many times have you seen a blurry shot of a crowded, bubbling sidewalk in a major city, only to see the shot change focus to reveal the sharp details?

Some other interesting ways to change focus include pulling from actors in one plane to reveal the subject of their attention in another (Figures 72.1–2). Picture a construction worker, then pull to reveal the bridge he is building. Or picture two cops in the background, and pull to reveal a bloody crime scene closer to the lens. How about a crowded city square bustling with blurry life until you pull to reveal your main character sitting in the foreground? A band onstage under a wash of pulsing, blurry lights as you quickly "snap" your focus to reveal the lead guitar player cranking out a nasty solo.

One last tip: Be thinking about the type of story you want to tell when you are ready to pull focus. Keep in mind that *the rate* of this move (how quickly or slowly you change focus) will also determine the type of story, and it should fit the style and genre in which you are working: Quick snaps in focus work less well for news than they do in music videos, and vice versa. Most important: Spend some time practicing. The more you know the particulars of how well your camera handles these adjustments, the better you will become at exploiting them to your advantage.

Figure 72.1

Figure 72.2

73 HOT WHEELS

It's no secret: Adding a flowing dolly or tracking shot to your project can crank up the production value, add a touch of class, deepen the visual storytelling potential, or all of the above. But there are some points to remember before you start rolling your camera and dragging your crew all over town.

The first thing to consider is this often overlooked question: Do I really need a complex dolly or tracking shot at this point in the story? I've seen the strongest professional crews wither when asked to set up dolly shot after dolly shot, especially if they find themselves on a rough or uneven surface and they spend day after day moving cumbersome track all over the place. If you can get away with a simple medium shot or you can move your actors first, consider it: Be wary of burning out your crew by dollying every shot. It's better to save their efforts for those moments that most demand this approach.

Second, too many shooters overlook the floor or surface that they intend to use for a dolly move. Be careful with this one. Obviously, for any rough surface, most outdoor locations, and on any floor that is uneven or tilted, you'll need to dolly on a track. Be sure to bring some wooden wedges along to even out any inconsistent areas or uneven pockets. Many floors that may be tiled or wooden can still cause issues. They may look smooth, but the smallest of gaps between tiles or planks can bring havoc on an otherwise "smooth" shot. Thin rugs, too, can hide imperfections that only the camera will pick up. Rugs also have a tendency to jockey wheels in odd, unexpected directions, even though the surface may appear smooth to the naked eye.

Outdoors, you'll need to search for uneven pavement, cracks in sidewalks, and foreign objects and trash that can send your shot into chaos in an instant. For shots on sand, grass, or other natural surfaces, track will work, but you can also try laying out several 4 x 8-foot panels to even out your ride. Always be on the lookout for a dolly rig that you can improvise: Wheelchairs, shopping carts, wagons, skateboards, and office chairs can all do the job (Figures 73.1–3).

Another solid idea is to keep a crate in your car full of extra materials that can help secure your camera to some of these types of rigs. After all, it doesn't matter how pretty the shot is if you crash your camera in the process. Fill your crate with a set of adjustable ratchet straps, some bungee cords, rope, wooden wedges, and anything else that might help you keep your gear secure. For those of you who are extra gung-ho to rig up a dolly, consider buying a tripod head that you can screw into a small plank of wood. By screwing a couple of handles into the board, you can strap the whole assembly in place, and safely roll to your heart's content. Got it? Good. Start rolling.

Figure 73.1

Figure 73.2

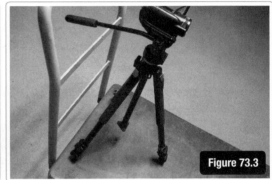

Figure 73.3

TIP74 STRAP IT UP

Now that you have this crate full of strange straps and ropes and stuff floating around in your trunk, what next? Well, now it's time to strap it up: your camera, that is. Prepare to strap it to cars, architecture, platforms, ladders, and almost any other secure surface to get that killer shot. Here's how.

Remember that plank of wood that I mentioned? It's the best investment I ever made. I took an old hunk of lumber, cut a scrap of thin carpet to fit it, and tacked the carpet onto one side. This helps prevent scratches when I strap the plank onto a car or a building. I attached two cheap handles from a hardware store and ran bungee cords (you can also use ratchet straps) through them to secure the plank. I then invested in a pro tripod head — just the head — and took it to a hardware store, where I matched the thread of a standard bolt to the hole in the base of the tripod head. Drilling through my plank, I stuck the bolt through, screwed my tripod head in place, and *voila*: I'm ready to rock (Figure 74.1).

With this rig in place, I can easily and safely shoot from the roof, hood, or side panels of a car; from the top of ladders or balconies; or strapped to an over-hang, archway, or bridge (Figure 74.2). I also keep a few scraps of foam core in my crate, which I wedge under the ratchet straps. This takes a little pressure off the straps and prevents damage to the surface. Total cost? Less than $200 (the tripod head alone was about $160). Total return? Killer shots from almost anywhere without endangering my gear, cast, or crew.

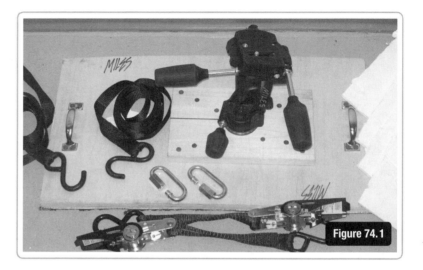

Figure 74.1

Figure 74.2

A note or two about car rigs (Figures 74.3–4): Check and recheck your straps. Make sure the whole rig doesn't slide around. Some shooters add a small clear piece of plastic to mount in front of their lens to protect it from stray rocks or other debris. Some prefer bigger rigs that use suction cups to attach to car panels. Also, and this is critical: Anytime you are shooting with a moving car, remember that speed is actually your enemy. Most moving shots look faster to the camera and to your viewers than normal motion. So there is rarely a need to drive faster than five to ten miles an hour *under* the speed limit. Pick lightly traveled roads, underused parking lots (Sundays are good days for this), streets without a lot of pedestrians, always making safety your top priority: I've yet to see a shot for which it was worth endangering yourself, your equipment, or your cast and crew.

Figure 74.3

My rig is designed for my camera. Renting an expensive (and heavy) camera and slapping it onto a flimsy rig is asking for trouble. Also, don't put yourself in a position to get injured while hitting "record." A big advantage of small cameras is the remote controls they often have: It's better to hit record while standing on the ground than while dangling over the side of a bridge. And if you *do* need to climb to hit record, take your time. Any additional footage that runs while you are climbing back down can be edited out later.

You can also consider securing your camera mounted traditionally on a tripod, but with the tripod legs *not* outwardly deployed. This works well when attaching the whole setup to a pole, balcony, railing, scaffolding, or other vertical (or linear) object using plastic zip ties. Lastly, if you have any doubt at all about the security of a setup, the position of a camera or your straps, or the overall safety of anyone involved (including random passersby), then bag the shot. You can always shoot the scene conventionally, without injury, damages, or worse: a costly and embarrassing lawsuit.

Figure 74.4

75 BACK IT UP

A group of my students approached me not long ago with a unique problem for an original short film they were producing. They needed to shoot a believable car accident, but wanted to make sure that things were done safely. After sketching out what they hoped to capture on paper, we came up with a superb plan for capturing the shot safely and effectively. Here's what we devised and how you can do it, too.

The plan was to shoot the entire sequence in reverse, at an extremely slow rate of speed, knowing that we could change the speed and direction of the footage during the edit. We set up the two cars that were meant to crash together in a wide, mostly empty parking lot, so that they met in a "T." The two cars were about five inches apart to start (Figure 75.1). The camera was placed atop one car, positioned so you could see the hood and the second car just beyond that (Figure 75.4). The actor driving the second car began the scene with his hands in the air, with a look of shock on his face (remember that the events were being shot in reverse). Then, with a few rehearsals and adjustments, both cars slowly rolled backwards, maybe reaching five miles per hour, and the actor switched from his look of shock to a normal driving position. And we rolled tape (Figures 75.2–3).

We also positioned several students in the parking lot to ensure that no other vehicles or pedestrians would enter a dangerous spot. And we shot three or four takes of this odd, slow, backwards sequence. I'll be honest: On-set it felt strange and awkward and most certainly looked ridiculous. But that was before the magic happened.

During the edit, we imported the shots, laid them into our time line, reversed the direction, and cranked up the speed — and it looked awesome! We only needed to adjust the speed once (too fast and it just looked silly) and add a "crashing" sound effect, and we had it! The whole thing took maybe two hours, without injury, property damage, or stress. I recommend that that you try the same thing for car crashes, certain fight scene moments, or even shots with weapons. (Check out Tip 81.)

Be advised: Check your editing software first to make sure that you can alter footage by changing the speed or by reversing the clip. Certain editing software actually does not allow these types of changes. And, as always, don't put your cars, actors, or crew in a position where they may be in danger. Use plastic weapons only; most toy stores have cheap stuff that actually looks real on camera. And be sure to rehearse any similar sequence in slow motion, walking through the action as needed, to make sure everyone knows how to execute the effect safely.

Figure 75.1

Figure 75.2

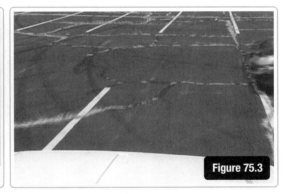

Figure 75.3

Figure 75.4

TIP 76
CHECKING THE OIL

Another quick, easy, and effective shot that you can add to your arsenal involves actually driving over your camera. And no, I don't mean in the "physically-crushing-it-beyond-recognition way," but actually driving so your vehicle straddles the camera position as it rests while capturing a low shot. Here are a few points to remember when you grab this memorable sequence (Figures 76.1–5).

The first thing you should ask yourself is this: Does this shot fit? In other words, is a highly stylized shot like this one appropriate for the type of story you are telling? This shot rocks for almost any action flick, cop movie, music video, or comedy. But it's tough to picture in a news piece, a documentary (unless it's about a race car driver), or a period drama. The next point to ponder is all about safety: Can I

Figure 76.1

Figure 76.2

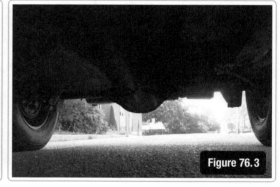

Figure 76.3

find a spot where I can set this up easily and safely? A big parking lot or a quiet stretch of road without a lot of pedestrians works well. Remember that speed kills and that any action (your car rolling along) will always look faster on screen than it is in real life, so there is no need to burn rubber. Take a few minutes to line this up correctly, so you don't actually end up crushing your own camera.

Finally, consider using the board that I described in previous chapters to mount the camera. Just check to make sure that you have clearance between the camera and the underside of the vehicle (Figure 76.6)! You can also try propping your camera on an old sweatshirt or a winter coat to lessen the chances that it will accidently fall or roll over. A small slice of plastic propped over the lens can help protect against stray rocks or debris. And don't expect to use the audio from this shot: The proximity of the car roaring overhead will probably blow out your on-camera mike, so leave time to record a second pass by the car, just for the purpose of capturing good audio. You can match this up with the visually satisfying take in editing.

For an extra layer of movie madness, shoot this stunning low angle twice, with the car traveling in each direction: once approaching the camera and again as you see the car driving away. By making a clean cut between the two during the edit, you should end up with a truly magnificent shot. Add bonus points for adding some groovy 1970s funk music on top of this sequence! Drive safely!

Figure 76.4

Figure 76.5

Figure 76.6

TIP 77
CLICK IT OR TRICK IT

As you may have already figured out, I'm a bit of a nerd regarding safety. I don't think any shot is worth endangering personnel or property, I think there is always time for a quick rehearsal, and I don't believe in taking poorly planned risks. Since I actually have had students get hit by cars while shooting, this is especially true for shots that involve driving. Fortunately, any vehicle that you choose to shoot from comes with the best safety feature you can use: a seat belt (Figure 77.1).

Relax. I'm not going to rant about wearing your seat belt when you drive, although, of course, you always should. Instead, I'm going to argue that you should strap your tripod in place before rolling (pun intended). I admit it: I once tried shooting video while I was driving, and man, was my mom angry! She hates driving with me as it is, much less when I'm rolling tape. So here's my advice: Don't do it.

If you really need that shot from inside the car — and the time will come when you will — here are a few great tips for shooting without getting into a wreck. First of all, the big secret about tripods is that the legs move independently. Normally, we try to extend all three legs to the same height. But if you need a shot of an actor driving a car, drop the tripod into the passenger seat, and fully extend two of the legs. These should run all the way down into the spot where you usually put human legs. Extend the third tripod leg halfway, and wedge it into the seat itself. Finish off this inexpensive setup by actually strapping the tripod in with the seat belt.

You should end up not only with a secure, snug setup for your camera that still allows you enough range of motion (with the tripod head) to get the shot, but also a second bonus. Too many amateur videos shot in cars bounce around too much. This is because they are shot handheld, and it's basically impossible to echo naturally the shakes and bumps that a car creates. By strapping the tripod down, the camera will automatically move in accordance with the vehicle, giving you pro-level shots that won't unintentionally give your audience motion sickness.

For a shot that grabs the point of view from the driver's seat, strap your tripod in the back, behind the driver's head, and zoom in just past his or her head to capture the shot (Figure 77.2). No matter how much actors beg, no matter how much they reassure you, don't let anyone drive and shoot at the same time, including yourself. If you do, my mother will surely track you down and let you know exactly what you're doing wrong. And she'll probably make you do your homework, too. Don't say I didn't warn you.

Figure 77.1

Figure 77.2

TIP 78
THUMBTACK HEAVEN

I've always loved sci-fi movies, and I've always loved finding out how they make sci-fi movies. And there's a super cheap, super simple, and highly effective sci-fi trick you can master without leaving your house. It's called a star field, and here's how you rock it.

Grab a black sheet of poster board, not too thick. Grab a thumbtack. Attack the poster board with the thumbtack in a highly random manner, creating a field of little holes with no visible pattern. Repeat as necessary. The result (Figure 78.1)? Not too impressive, at least until you put a light behind it! You can use almost any intense light with a fairly narrow pool, such as a desk lamp. Prop the poster board up vertically, taping it or clamping it in place. You can use an open-back chair, an empty picture frame, or anything that's vertical, sturdy, and stable. Put the lamp about two feet behind the poster board (Figure 78.2). How's it looking? Better, but not brilliant?

Now for the real magic. Set your camera up to point directly at the tagboard on the opposite side from the light. You should make sure to frame tightly enough so you don't see the edges of the black board. Now look again, this time through the viewfinder. Awesome, right? There's just something stunning about the way the camera captures this simple scenario: The tiny pinholes start to glisten and gleam like real stars, some out of focus, some in focus. You can add another layer by grabbing different-colored sheets of lighting gel and taping them to the back of the poster. The hints of blue, green, and red that pop through, with a little imagination, will start to transport you to another galaxy.

So what's it good for? It's great for shots of starships or those action figures you have in a box in the basement (Figure 78.3). You can also use this setup to increase the visual sparkle (pun intended) of product shots, to create an interesting background for graphics, or to show off that trophy that your softball team won last spring. The possibilities are almost as limitless as… (sorry, I can't help it) the cold vastness of space itself! Go! Go, brave space traveler! Reach for the stars. Or at least for a thumbtack.

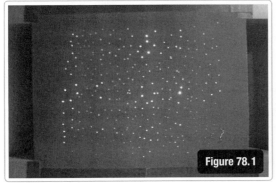

Figure 78.1

Figure 78.2

Figure 78.3

TIP 79
TELLING IT STRAIGHT

A big problem that I see all too often involves shooting interviews, establishing proper eye lines, and selecting the best framings. Address each of these three key problems one at a time, and you'll start shooting quality interviews right away.

First of all, a successful interview shoot starts with solid preparation. You should do some research on your subjects: their background, habits, hobbies or work status, and characteristics that make them interesting, controversial, or informative. Write your questions in advance, but be willing to drift from this list as the interview rolls along. More established subjects (politicians, performers, administrators, athletes) may require advance copies of the questions. Make sure you let them know what colors and outfits will work best on-camera, that bringing an extra set of clothes is never a bad idea, and that they may need to wear a wireless mike (if you use one with your camera rig). Get permission in writing, in advance if possible, for them to appear in your project.

In terms of the shoot itself, try to shoot indoors whenever possible. Unless your subject is a logger or a lifeguard, stay indoors: It's just easier to control the various elements (audio, background elements, and so forth). Find a quiet interior where you and your subject can each sit comfortably (see more below). Be sure to set up so that the background offers good contrast to your subject (see the previous tip on patterns and colors). Make sure phones are off and doors are closed whenever possible. Leave yourself some extra time before and after the scheduled interview. Before starting, you may need to run power cables, move a plant, close some blinds, or make other adjustments. Extra time afterward allows you to pack up the gear but also serves as padding in case your subject is extra talkative and you need to keep rolling.

Eye lines can be a little tricky to master, but are crucial to getting your interviews to look as slick as possible. Rule number one: Make sure your camera is vertically at eye level with the subject. This is key: You don't want to imply a superior or inferior position with relation to the subject by shooting up or down, even slightly. Rule number two: Make sure you and your subject sit in nearly identical chairs so you can maintain eye contact comfortably and the interviewee won't be looking up or down, which always appears awkward. Rule number three: Place your chair as close to the lens as possible, but still just a touch off to one side. If you are (hopefully!) using three-point lighting, this chair should be positioned on the same side as the key light. This will ensure that the subject's eye line will appear (to the viewer) to fall just to the side of the lens, a touch off center (Figure 79.1). In general, if interviewees' eyes drift too far off, they seem disconnected to the viewer; and if they stare directly into the lens, they can seem too powerful.

Another key piece of advice: Move your camera close to the subject. This feels awkward to new shooters, and some subjects, and, yes, you could simply zoom in tighter. But physically moving the camera closer always results in a better image. This brings us to the framings themselves. You will rarely need to be wider than a medium shot (again, the viewer feels disconnected). With a medium, you can shoot basically the entire piece. For variety, try tightening in to a medium

close-up or a head shot, but wait to zoom closer until the subject finishes speaking. I generally shoot the first third of an interview in a medium, then adjust to the tighter framings for the final two thirds. When I'm on my game, I bunch my simple questions up front (medium shot), and save my more pressing or "serious" questions for the tighter, more intimate, framings.

One last note: Decide in advance if you want your viewers to hear *you* asking the questions. Some shows work this way, but many do not. If you don't want the questions in the final piece, make sure to leave a few seconds between every question, answer, and subsequent question. This can also take getting used to, but it's worth it in the end.

Figure 79.1

TIP 80
BENNY HILL VS. PRIVATE RYAN

Playing with frame rates and shutter speeds can be rewarding, but can also yield a high degree of frustration. This tip may prove difficult, depending on what camera you are using and how much control it offers over these functions. A large number of camcorders now feature minimal control over shutter speed or frame rate, but you may only see slight variations in your image, and these may be difficult to alter. But you should play anyway and see how far you can take your gear in producing a variety of results.

Remember that frame rate and shutter speed are different effects (Tip 7). It's important to recall that fast motion and slow motion involve different frame rates: the number of frames exposed per second. Video runs at thirty frames per second (fps). With fast motion, or time-lapse footage, you actually shoot fewer frames, and for slow motion you add frames (think of it as adding information). Many types of editing software offer the option to change clip speed, but this process works differently than it does in-camera. The main things to determine are: (1) does your camera offer these features; and (2) is a change in frame rate or shutter speed the best option to tell a given story?

Either way, spend some time shooting practice footage to see how these changes alter the image with your particular camera. I would also suggest shooting test footage and then altering those clips during the editing process. Then the only thing left is to be honest about the results: Are the images that you manipulated doing what you envisioned? Is this particular effect valid for the project? The stunning battle scenes in *Saving Private Ryan*, for example, exemplify a brilliant use of varied shutter speeds, while the comedy chases in *The Benny Hill Show* rely on changes in frame rate.

There are tons of fun applications for altered frame rates. One trick that I love is to place subjects in a crowded, busy environment, and then ask them not to move as their world flies past. By speeding up the footage, they appear to stay still while the madness spins past. For more impact, have them sit in a big, comfy chair — bonus points for putting this chair on a beach, a busy city sidewalk, or in a bustling shopping mall. Time-lapse shots work great for shooting big action, like a stadium filling up, a construction site in full gear, or a rock band setting up for a concert. If your camera shoots time-lapse, this is even easier. Remember to lock off your camera and control the recording with your remote.

During your edit, don't be afraid to further alter the images. I did some time-lapse test footage recently of a band onstage at a local club. By slowing down the footage at the end of the clip, I generated a moment that increased the visual and storytelling weight.

For slow-motion work, I love seeing sports clips and action shots in a slower format. Keep in mind, of course, that adding camera movement to a shot with altered speeds is more complicated. But, as always, I encourage you to go play, practice, try new things, and take some risks. Your viewers (and hopefully your clients) will dig it.

TIP 81
BACK INTACT

A lot of beginning filmmakers and students gravitate toward making action and horror films, full of fistfights, bloody faces, and weapons of all sorts. It is worth reviewing a few tips for dealing with weapons that both ensure the safety of everyone involved, and also help your videos become more believable and effective.

First of all, if you shoot scenes that include weapons of any kind, you must take as many precautions as possible to maintain safety. *You should never use actual weapons in your films*. Period. No matter how safe you think they are. Also, even if you are using the softest, safest toy or prop weapon that you can get your hands on, you should never ask actors to perform an action that they are uncomfortable completing or that they have not rehearsed (always run a few half-speed rehearsals of any complex action before shooting). If your weapons are fake guns, I strongly recommend telling the police that you will be shooting such a scene and displaying large signs (outside of the frame) that let passersby know that what they are seeing isn't real. A good friend of mine ended up with a cop pointing a *real* gun at his head while shooting a robbery scene in a deli. It's an experience he doesn't ever want anyone else to share.

So you have your rubber machete or sword and a bunch of folks dressed up like zombies, and you're ready to shoot the scene in which the hero grabs a knife and throws it across the room into the chest of the biggest, baddest zombie of them all. How can you pull this shot off successfully? There are two main techniques. The first tip involves a classic use of the whip pan, in which actors get "shot" with arrows, spears, or a knife. The first half of the whip should show your hero throwing the weapon. The second part "sells" the effect by whipping to the zombie, which implies that the weapon is streaking through the air. This shot whips to the zombie, who already has a prop knife "stuck" in his chest or head. This is actually a plastic prop, cut in half and taped in place through a small hole in the costume, ideally soaking in a wash of fake blood. The two shots combined with a gruesome sound effect will delight your viewers.

A second trick involves reverse footage. In this instance, you want to attach a length of fishing line to the prop weapon, like an arrow. You start the shot with the arrow nestled between the victim's arm and torso; then, as you roll, a crew member yanks on the fishing line, pulling the prop away from the actor. With good timing and a little acting, you can reverse the clip later to make your audience feel like they just saw the arrow zip into the actor's chest. Add a simple sound effect to complete the trick.

TIP 82

BIFF! POW! BLAM!

Everybody loves a good punch-up, at least in the movies. But before you roll out to the backyard with your friends to shoot your epic, macho, tough-guy flick, there are a few precautions you should take so no one actually gets banged up.

Pulling off good fight scenes safely is a combination of actor placement, camera placement, and a dash of solid sound effects. The first guideline to follow is that at no point should any actor actually strike another actor. I know this seems obvious, but even in the most brilliant fight scenes, from *The Bourne Identity* to *Gladiator*, the actors aren't really taking it on the chin. They work through each sequence slowly and carefully before rolling, to ensure that everyone knows when and where fists will be flying.

The second crucial aspect to understand is that safe, believable fight scenes almost always involve a concept called "hiding the punch." In other words, you should always look to place an actor *between* the camera and the impact, allowing you to avoid having your actors actually hit each other and letting the imagination and the sound effects fool the viewer. It's all about tricking the eye. For example, with a simple right cross, placing the actor who gets hit with his back to the camera hides the punch thrown by a second actor. A good rule of thumb is always to allow about a foot of clearance between hands and faces: A camera behind the punched actor will "flatten" this distance, and with a swift turn of the head, the punch looks real.

A standard technique for punches and slaps that builds on this setup involves having the actors who will be "hit" hold their hand in front of their face, turned to the side. This offers a flat target for the actor who is punching and guarantees that the swing will land *in front* of the other performer's face, not on it (Figures 82.1–3). Also, as with vehicles, speed kills: There's no need to run most fight scenes at 100%. Not only will the camera cause the action to appear faster, but you can subtly accelerate the clip while editing to add speed.

For body blows and stomach kicks, use this same setup (Figures 82.4–6). Again, the actors being hit should keep their hands in front of them, offering a target and adding a layer of self-preservation to the action. The second actor gently makes contact with the palms of the first actor without risking injury. For more dramatic kicks, include a whip pan: The swift motion tends to hide the fact that no contact is actually occurring. This is also true of elbows, backhand hits, and other blows. Keep in mind that the icing on the fight cake is actually just making sure that the actors being hit are snapping back from the impact, selling the hit to the viewers by their reactions.

As a final note, sometimes combining two shots tightly in an edit helps hide the absence of contact. Take another look at those sword fights from *Gladiator*. The editing hides 90% of the actual combat, giving you instead a blur of action and a heavy dose of sound effects to achieve the desired results.

As for sound, I cover a lot of the techniques later in the book (see Tip 94). But for now, you can find a lot of effective audio clips online, and for those of you intending to do more advanced editing, I recommend investing in a set of sound effects CDs.

Figure 82.1

Figure 82.2

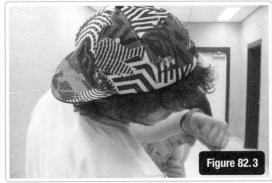

Figure 82.3

Figure 82.4

Figure 82.5

Figure 82.6

TIP 83
ARCH VILLAINS AND ARCH HEROES

By now you should officially be fed up with the limitations of our old friend the frame. It's not big enough, it forces your hand, it's predictable. But another fantastic technique is here to save you, a simple trick that captivates viewers and works in almost any genre. I'm talking about a tried-and-true method of composing images called "the frame within the frame," and it's so simple and elegant that it works for films, music videos, art-house films, documentaries, instructional videos — you name it.

Jot down a quick list of all the different types of frames that you can think of: picture frames, doors, (Figure 83.1), windows, arches, bridges, rusted-out sheets of metal, tree limbs, fences; the list goes on and on. By carefully placing actors or objects within these naturally occurring frames, you can organically and memorably break up that boring old rectangle that has been defining your work up to this point (Figure 83.2).

Don't believe me? Set your camera up; it doesn't matter where. Frame up on an ordinary object, say, a can of soda. Pretty dull, huh? Now grab an everyday item that almost anyone has lying around: books. Take two books and stand them on end in the foreground of the shot, leaving the soda can in the middle or background in the gap between the edges of the two books. Bang! Instantly, you've "chopped up" the boring original framing, creating three rectangles (one on each side plus one created by the space between them).

Still don't buy it? Grab a friend and your camera and head outside. Practice placing your friend in a few simple doorways, another easily discovered frame within the frame. In fact, anything that acts in this "cookie-cutter" manner, slicing the frame into unexpected shapes, can work wonders for you.

Think of the possibilities: an actor walking into an open doorway, the camera moving to a "break" in a fence line, two actors "separated" (physically and symbolically) by physical slices in space. Coupling this technique by placing the actor in silhouette (lit from behind, showing only the darkened outline of the subject) cranks thing up a few more notches. It's a breathtaking way to break up the usual shots and compositions, and it's a trick that's only limited by the types of frames that you discover around you.

Can't find anything in your neighborhood? Don't hesitate to use anything and everything at your disposal to create frames: open-back chairs, those cheap metal book holders from the library, gaps in a line of books on a bookshelf, windows, interior doors left slightly open, even a sheet of poster board that you carve into an interesting shape. I guarantee, once you start seeing the unlimited uses for this trick, you'll find a way to work it into your videos again and again.

Figure 83.1

Figure 83.2

EXERCISE

TEN BY TEN, ADVANCED TECHNIQUES

BE SURE TO MASTER THESE ADVANCED TRICKS WITH PRACTICE, PRACTICE, AND MORE PRACTICE.

1. Practice continuity of action by shooting two friends walking into your house from the street, using different framings. Make sure that both actors maintain proper screen direction (traveling right to left, for example) and that their actions are the same from framing to framing.

2. Break out an old family album and shoot a sequence of your favorite family photos. Try simulating camera moves (pans and tilts) by zooming in and then slowly moving the photo past the camera lens.

3. Head for a long hallway, parking lot, or a large, open room. Set up three different ordinary objects (bottles, soda cans, vases, for example), one each in the foreground, middle, and background. Practice pulling focus between them, making sure that *only one* of the objects is sharp at any given point.

4. What do you mean you didn't build a star field yet? Get with it!

5. Grab a willing friend, buy him or her lunch, and then head for a park or a quiet street. Shoot a simple action, like your pal walking left to right in the shot. Repeat this several times as you make adjustments to the shutter speed (now you know why you buy lunch *first*). Reset this scene and make adjustments to the frame rate. Be sure to watch the footage later to see the different results. For a quick and easy way to keep track of the various settings, write them on a dry erase board that your friend holds in the shot.

6. On the next warm, sunny day, grab your tripod and practice wedging it into the passenger seat. Don't forget to use the seat belt! Once you're wedged, go ahead and take a test spin, rolling some test footage on the way.

7. Interview a teacher, friend, family member, or coworker. It doesn't really matter what you ask them about, although it will help if they talk about something interesting. The bigger point is to get the eye lines correct and to practice finding three different framings for a single interview.

8. Shoot nine different frames within the frame: three that you find in your house, three that you find somewhere in your neighborhood, on campus, or in town, and three that you make out of unusual items or materials.

9. Appropriate some random wheels and practice improvising dolly shots. Bonus points if your boyfriend or girlfriend works at a local supermarket.

10. At the risk of upsetting my publisher, his lawyers, or both, practice punching your best friend in the face. There. I said it. Just **please**, **please**, **please** use the safety measures and camera setups that I described. And if anyone *does* accidentally get popped in the schnoz, please don't sue us. Thanks.

SECTION 7

EDITING ▶

TIP 84
VIVE LE MONTAGE!

You're almost at the point where you can put down the camera and focus on editing tricks: image and audio manipulations to amp up your videos. As noted, certain tricks exist entirely in the camera or in the lighting setup, but as you progress, you'll need to think about shooting as part one of editing, and editing as part two of shooting.

This idea is important when dealing with a classic cinematic technique: the montage. Montage is the French word for *assembly* and is understood to mean a group of like things put together in an interesting way. In film, we see two general approaches to montage: the intensification of action and the intensification of an idea. Both assemble a sequence of shots that compress time and space in a pleasing way, allowing the audience (and the character) to move ahead quickly in the story. But don't let this simple idea fool you: The two are very different. Let's deal with intensification of an idea first.

This is certainly a trickier notion. After all, what is this big idea, anyway? It could be a feeling, a sense of tone, or an emotional change in the character. Either way, this method tends to be more abstract, relying on well-developed images to evoke a certain emotional reaction among the viewers or an emotional shift in the characters. But be careful: Just slapping a few shots together over a bed of music can cause you to slide into cheesy territory rather quickly (see almost the entire body of films from the 1980s).

In other words, you need to pick your shots, and the actions or emotions that those shots reveal, very carefully. Be prepared to shoot with one idea in mind only to discover an alternative sequence that's more effective while you are editing. You almost have to get to a point where that other half of your brain takes over and you judge the sequence less on how it was written or performed and more on how the overall series flows together to bring you and your audience to a unique place.

Easy, right? Not so much. Maybe it helps if you are French? But I know that this style of montage tends to work most effectively with drama, end of story. It's tough to pull off in a straight comedy, documentary, or cooking show. And I also see too many music videos trying to exploit montage, but just ending up as a sequence of nice shots. In fact, rough edits (where an early draft of the sequence is roughly stuffed into place on an editing time line) are often called assembly edits; they really are just raw shots in a line. Remember, the point is that the idea, the feeling, grows in intensity. Get it right, and you might just be ready to call yourself a filmmaker.

TIP 85
LESS IS MORE

Let's take a look at the other style of montage: intensification of action. As before, this approach can be incredibly powerful, but can also teeter on the brink of cheese if you aren't careful. Just think about most sports films and you'll understand what I mean. They always end up showing us that sequence where the home team just can't win or just can't lose in a quick series of shots with an up-tempo musical track underneath. Hoo boy. We can do better than that, right?

This is where the concept of less is more truly comes into play. It's tempting to shoot and edit a montage of all kinds of action, from the very simple to the more abstract and extended. This can be a captivating style of filmmaking. Think of those action flicks in which the hero assembles his team and they busy themselves with the complex machinations of planning the big heist. The *Ocean's Eleven* series does this masterfully, and it's great fun. But Soderbergh always knows when to turn off the jets. And his cuts are super, super tight, showing us just enough information, creating a fabric and a rhythm that keeps our attention.

My favorite example of how the less-is-more principle helps to guide this style of montage comes from *The Shawshank Redemption*. In a series of only five shots (Figures 85.1–5), the audience feels as if Tim Robbins' character has struggled to survive several brutal years behind bars. Five shots! Another great example, this time from a comedy, comes in the opening sequences for the hilarious *Talladega Nights: The Ballad of Ricky Bobby*, in which the lead character whips with us from the racetrack to the winner's circle to pit row and around again. And a fantastically informative montage fills the first portion of the documentary, *A League of Ordinary Gentlemen*, where the viewer is quickly shown the history of professional bowling and its fall from broadcasting grace.

In all of these examples, the director and editor worked together to keep a simple concept, the intensification of action, from becoming cumbersome. The viewer receives just the right amount of information as the action and the story unfold. As you begin to experiment with both forms of montage, remember that you will be jumping through space and time, and you will find success on the other side if you plan to shoot memorable images, keep an open mind during the edit, and, above all, obey the golden rule: In film and video, less really is more.

Figure 85.1

Figure 85.2

Figure 85.3

Figure 85.4

Figure 85.5

™86 PAPER DEMONS

A crucial skill that you will want to master actually has nothing to do with cameras, tripods, editing software, or lighting. It's all on paper, baby, and it's a skill that just might get you hired in this crazy business.

I'm talking paper edits, logging footage before you begin actually importing clips. I know this may seem like a huge waste of time, and for a short project that only takes half of a Mini DV tape, *maybe* you can skip this step. But I guarantee that for longer projects, like films, or if you break into editing sports highlights or news or producing for TV, you'll need to master this important skill.

The good news is that, in its simplest form, it's mad easy. Logging sheets are essentially a record of every single shot on a piece of tape or on a hard disk, from a particular shoot (Figure 86.1). You note the exact time code, the type of shot, camera angle, or framing, a fragment of dialogue, and any critical aspects. These might include bad audio (airplanes overhead), swear words (not good for kids' shows) or glitches with the shot (lighting, camera moves). For films, you will note any poor takes, blown stunts, or improvised dialogue. Some films rely on a script supervisor to note these aspects, and most directors have them circle the best takes on-set, so that by the time you get the footage, you already have a rough idea of which clips to use.

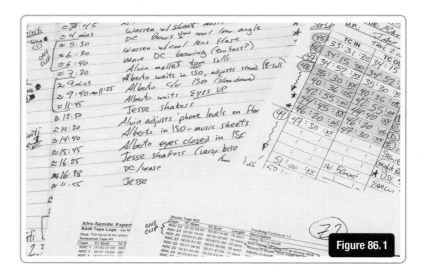

Figure 86.1

Another crucial reason for marking down what shots are valuable and what shots are already ruined is the idea of saving hard drive space, reducing the number of clips, or simply saving time. If you're making short videos, hard drive space issues probably won't creep up, at least not on a single project. You also probably won't be wrangling with a huge number of clips or a time crunch. But once you jump into a professional environment, all of these things become very important (also remember that logging is a crucial entry-level skill at most pro production companies or TV shows).

The other key skill that logging forces you to develop and that will serve you well when you go pro is the ability to make editing decisions on paper. For example, if you shot a twenty-five-minute interview, the first few minutes might just be "throwaway" questions that you and your producer will never use. So why import them? Also, especially for longer projects or those that generate a lot of footage, logging gets you familiar with the total body of work. You never know when your editor may be deep in a montage and need a certain extra something to make the sequence work, something that maybe wasn't in the script or even on a shot list, but that you will be able to provide, simply because you've seen it: It's in your logs.

Your logs can also provide the editor or director with an edit decision list, which is the next step. The logs reveal everything that was shot, and the edit list highlights those takes or clips that are the most valuable. To start, use a simple sheet of lined paper or a spreadsheet program. The format doesn't matter as much as going through the process. Once you have some footage logged, you can turn them into an edit decision list by *literally highlighting* the selections that are most important. If you're feeling *really* fancy, you can find templates for both documents online in about three seconds. Now, grab some of the footage that you have already shot and start logging!

TIP 87
LINKS IN THE CHAIN

With editing, two often misunderstood techniques can help solve a multitude of problems, forming key links in the chain of your project. These two techniques, B-roll and voice over, can patch up a rough edit, cover up a strange shot, or bring crucial information to your viewers that didn't make it into the camera during production.

B-roll is a news term that generally describes any *additional* footage that is used to tell the story. The name comes from the ancient, mysterious practice of editing using two analog video tape decks to assemble the edit. The decks each held a roll of tape, the "A" roll featuring on-camera footage of the reporter or any eyewitnesses and the "B" roll providing additional footage. This is usually comprised of secondary shots of exteriors, signs, locations, crowds, close-ups, events, or other actions that help tell the story. And this is the crucial part: additional footage that *helps to tell the story*. B-roll is not just a random assortment of shots, although most news stations and production companies tend to keep a stock of generic footage on hand to help beef up stories (footage of folks at the beach, for example, for a story about a heat wave).

And you should also know that B-roll doesn't physically have to come from a second roll of tape. Most pro shooters and field producers will slam as much secondary footage on a single tape or video card after getting their interviews in the can. It can come from a variety of sources. Companies, schools, and sports teams these days all tend to keep a video library that can be a source of footage

(be sure to get permission). You may not use this concept in dramas or comedies, but you will come to depend on it if you shoot documentaries, news, or "man in the street" style video.

The voice over (VO) is a second valuable tool that can save you in an edit. To be clear, most professionals aim for fiction pieces that avoid either voice over or narration (provided by a character or a narrator). In fact, the old adage in film tells us to show our audience what is important, not tell them. And films can suffer from tacked-on voice over, which plugs awkward gaps in the story or the performances. But if you are shooting nonfiction (news, sports, documentaries), voice over is a respected, traditional method to broadcast information.

This doesn't mean that you should just plug in the mike and start yapping away. I ask my TV news students to write and rewrite and then rewrite again before recording their voice overs. You want to keep your message simple, clear, and informative. For a truly professional result, be sure to lay out an edit that is as close to final as possible *before* tracking audio for a voice over. You may find that a simple shot tells viewers all they need to know or that a few simple words, written and spoken well, can better complete the piece. You can record voice overs in-camera or with a separate mike straight into the computer (depending on your editing software, you may need to separate or combine audio and video tracks). In either case, don't forget that the term truly means that the *voice* works *over* the images. You should always match your words to the picture.

TIP 88

L AND J

No matter how basic or complex your editing skills are, your videos can benefit from two advanced techniques called L and J edits. These are actually pretty simple, but often trip people up when they tackle them initially. The best way to master them is to read the descriptions, and then shoot some tape and practice. Editing software platforms vary to a large degree, so concentrate on the overall concept and then explore how to execute it with the particular setup or system you are using.

To grasp these two editing styles, you need to picture a clip on the layout in most editing setups: You should see strips or bands of media files that correspond to clips of video with accompanying audio. They may be different colors or lengths or in varying numbers (for example, you may have two tracks of stereo audio). Generally, the audio and video are (at least) two separate strips of media, set on top of one another like layers on a cake. Next, picture (or place on your time line) a second, unrelated clip beside this first set of media. For instance, the first clip might be an exterior shot and the second clip might be two characters inside that location, speaking in a conference room. Once you have this rough edit in place, you can start cutting.

To create an L edit, you need to make the shapes of these media files appear like an "L": the audio track runs longer than the video track, stretching to the right like the lower line of the letter "L" (Figure 88.1). You do this by cutting *only* the video track. The result will be that the sound from the shot continues beyond the length of the image. By then placing a second shot above this audio, the original sound continues "underneath" the image (visually, in the software) and the audio from one image flows into the next shot.

As you might guess, a J edit works exactly the same way but in reverse, with two clips altered so that the audio *begins before* the next shot (Figure 88.2). This is an incredibly powerful tool, forcing your viewers to hear the audio from the upcoming shot while still digesting the current on-screen image. A classic example of these edits in film involves a train whizzing by the camera, blasting its whistle as it passes. In an L edit, the whistle would continue to scream into the next shot or scene, causing a jarring effect. In a J edit, a character who is about to take a trip may be shown as we hear the whistle, but before we see the train, echoing the urgent need to travel that is felt by that character. Again, use your best judgment, especially with regard to what genre you are shooting, when deciding when to use these editing tricks. They work great in films, for both dramas and comedy, but can also be effective with news or sports.

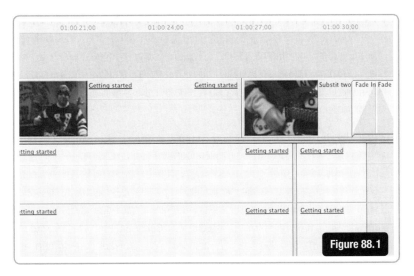

Figure 88.1

Figure 88.2

89 FONT YOU!

When you first start adding fonts, graphics, and still images to your edits, you may, in fact, be entering a world of hurt. Despite the fact that many beginning-level editing platforms have improved their abilities to import photos and generate text, many otherwise great videos suffer from fonts that don't export cleanly, images that ghost, and graphics that, well, just look cheesy. Don't worry: I'm here to help.

Let's look at fonts first. To begin with, make sure that the fonts you want to use are installed on your machine and are displaying properly *within* the editing software. Next, I suggest making a quick thirty-second video using clips from your practice tape, adding fonts, exporting this as a file, and making sure that the fonts display in the outputted format. If you really step it up or are using an advanced editing program, I suggest that you slap a quick "dummy" video together and practice manipulating the font generator(s) to get the results that you want.

Most basic editing programs will push you towards using their pre-installed set of fonts, giving you varying degrees of control over the color, size, and placement of the words you want to add, which is convenient. But be careful. More and more videos have been posted with these pre-set elements. If you simply need to post a video quickly, don't worry. But if you are putting the finishing touches on your master work or your epic film, you may want to invest some more time in generating customized fonts or full graphics. In any case, gather the courage to gravitate away from the pre-set fonts. Remember that your video might also benefit from a timeless, classic treatment of on-screen words: plain white text on a black background. Avoid switching fonts numerous times during the same project: You'll lose views because of this easy trap.

A professional application of customized fonts or graphics that works in a number of genres and helps to inform viewers is called a lower third (Figures 89.1 and 3). This is a strip of color or a subtle pattern that runs along the bottom third of the screen and serves as an eye-catching spot to run text. The beautiful thing about a lower third is that it fits nicely in a frame that includes a person, either at waist level (mediums) or under the chin (head shots), allowing viewers to read the identity and often the location of the subject. You've seen this used on the news for ages. If you produce news-style videos, mastering this is a must. Many of the newer software applications have one pre-build, and most look great. In the advanced versions of editing software, you may need to take a few extra steps to make these work, including moving the text from a centered position to sit along the lower third (you *do* remember the rule of thirds, right?), but it's worth the effort.

When dealing with still images or pictures, the newest out-of-the-box software is much improved. Most of these applications can handle a variety of file types, from JPEGs to PICTs to pictures copied directly from the camera. In advanced applications, I encourage you to save your stills as PICT files, which tend to work better in pro-grade editing platforms. PICTs also render fonts correctly (Figure 89.2) and present transparent elements in images with better accuracy. In creating images, or altering them for video, keep in mind that you will want them to appear in the correct aspect ratio, without stretching, and a number of the better image editing programs now contain a pre-set for the correct video screen size when creating a new file. You should make every effort to learn how to create the correct file type and file size before importing photos into your editing software. You should also decide if you want to make a lower third or a full screen "card" to use in your video (Figure 89.4). In either case, make sure you render the fonts in the photo editing program *first*, and then run a test of the edit with the graphic(s) included before continuing with the project.

CAP'N WILL
✤ CONVERSATIONS
✤ DESTINATIONS
✤ LIBATIONS

Figure 89.1

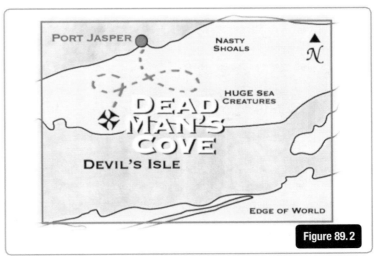

PORT JASPER
NASTY SHOALS
HUGE SEA CREATURES
DEAD MANS COVE
DEVIL'S ISLE
EDGE OF WORLD
N

Figure 89.2

HARTFORD WHALERS
HARTFORD WHALERS
SAVE
Dave Schneider
defenseman/guitarist/singer

Figure 89.3

YJTV NEWS CH. 19
LITICS EDUCATION HEAL
THER NEWS CLUBS POLIT
WEATHER NEWS CLUBS P

Figure 89.4

TIP 90
TO WIPE OR NOT TO WIPE

Transitions are another set of sand traps that new video gurus fall into far too often. Circle wipes, cube wipes, page peels, ripples, and weird dissolves — most of these come pre-set in many of the current editing software applications. Unless you use them for a very particular purpose, you're on the express bus to Cheeseville.

Fancy transitions give your video an amateur air because they call attention to themselves. The secret to a good edit, any time you elect to cut or to cross-fade, is to keep the edit as seamless as possible, helping your audience maintain the illusion of disbelief. Funny wipes and crazy fades only give them a reason to look *at the edit* and not continue to take the visual journey. A good rule of thumb is to cut only when necessary and to cross-fade only when a cut doesn't work.

There are, of course, exceptions to this rule. Especially in comedies, a ripple dissolve is a standard method for announcing a flashback or dream sequence to the audience. Cross-fades almost always imply a change in time. Fading to black and then fading back in does this as well, especially if your character is in the same location for both clips. Speaking of clips, be sure to import more footage for each clip than you think you need. Most nonlinear digital editing programs actually use additional frames from each clip to complete the effect. In other words, a fade between two clips isn't an extra element that is placed on top of the clips (even if it appears as an icon on your screen that sits between

them). It's more like a command to the program to reach past the in or out point for each clip and then blend those frames together.

One method to avoid standard transitions, called a screen wipe, is executed first in production and then finished in the edit. Let's say you are shooting a scene and you are completing a wide shot. To transition to a medium framing, have an actor walk very close to the camera at the tail end of the wide shot (Figures 90.1–2). Then, at the beginning of the medium shot, have the same actor repeat this move at the start of the shot (Figure 90.3). You may need a couple of takes to get the timing right, but it's worth it: You should end up with a blur that slides across the screen in both clips. By cutting on this movement, the screen "wipes" in an interesting way, and you end up with a slick transition that feels like it is a natural part of the action.

Another way that this type of edit is frequently used involves wiping off common objects that pass across the frame. Picture two characters at a café. Two different framings of this scene can be wiped together as cars in the street pass by the camera, blurring the image in a number of interesting ways with dashes of color. You can create these transitions from objects, crowds, props, architecture, almost anything that blurs across your frame (Figure 90.4). And you don't need a cheesy wipe to make it happen!

Figure 90.1

Figure 90.2

Figure 90.3

himself
a man"
JOHNSON

Figure 90.4

EXERCISE

TEN BY TEN, MEASURE TWICE, CUT ONCE

HERE ARE SOME FUNKY EXERCISES TO HELP YOU GET YOUR EDITING GROOVE ON.

1. I know, I know. It sounds boring. But take your footage from the other exercises in this book, find or make a logging sheet, and write down every shot. Just do it.

2. Try a basic idea montage. Remember, this is essentially showing an emotion, feeling, or thought growing or developing. This could be a character falling in love, deciding to quit her job, or trying to crack a decades-old murder case. Try to show this idea developing in less than ten shots.

3. Here's an "easier" montage challenge: Master the action montage, again in less than ten shots. This could feature characters fixing up an old car, practicing slap shots so they can make the hockey team, or (my personal favorite) trying to finish writing a book without pushing back their deadline sixty-three times.

4. Put together a two-minute edit using random clips that you have already shot. Write and then record a voice over that tells a coherent story using this footage.

5. News time! Pick an interesting event, story, development, or issue like gas prices, your school dress code, or a national holiday. Shoot five minutes of B-roll and edit this down to a two-minute news story.

6. With your completed news story, try adding some basic graphics. Make sure they are relevant to the content. For example, you could build a lower third to reveal information about a particular location. Next, create two full screen graphics that serve as title cards for your montage videos.

7. Go back to the footage you shot of some basic sequences and re-edit these clips to include an L and a J edit. If they don't work with the clips you already have, run out and pop a shot or two to make these edits work.

8. Shoot a basic scene with one actor explaining a dream she or he recently had to another actor. Then go ahead — why not? Add that ripple dissolve into the edit to transition to the dream sequence. Next stop: Cheeseville!

9. Shoot a wide exterior shot and a medium interior shot of an actor in a living room. Blend these two shots together using a traditional cross-fade. Then, and here's the funky part, *adjust the duration of the fade* to see how changing this aspect affects the mood, tone, or feeling of the piece.

10. Set up a "restaurant" scene (this can be in your own kitchen) with two actors sharing a meal together. Try creating different screen wipes to cut between framings (wide to medium, for instance). These can be made with a third actor playing a waiter who passes by the lens. Remember: It's all about the timing.

SECTION 8
AUDIO ▶

TIP 91
THESE BOOTS ARE MADE FOR TALKING

Audio issues doom more films and videos than bad acting, flimsy sets, or boring scripts. A bad film with good audio is much more watchable than a good film with bad audio. And, as the truism goes, 90% of what you *think* you see on screen is actually what you hear. The power of good audio can't be stressed enough, so let's jump into some great tricks for improving your audio.

The first thing to understand, as with editing, is that you *can* fix a number of audio issues after the movie is shot. For big Hollywood flicks, special performers called foley artists add sounds to the action on the screen and fill in little sounds that complete the overall sonic atmosphere. Understand that most big films are shot with almost no on-set noises, with foley artists filling in the gaps, and you'll know what I mean. For example, if your two big stars shoot a dialogue scene in a restaurant, almost all the incidental noises (clinking glasses, murmuring patrons, scrapping silverware) are added after the fact. This is all to ensure that the dialogue gets recorded cleanly during production and to help isolate and control the various audio elements during the edit.

Foley stages are special sound environments that come complete with a variety of surfaces (to record footsteps), bizarre gadgets, hand-me-down trinkets (for clinks and clanks and dings), and a maddening array of typewriters, old phones, creaking desks, and other props to bring screen action to life. Once your video is done (especially in the case of dramatic films or other fiction projects), get ready to embrace your inner foley artist.

The best advice I can give you is to invest in a good microphone. Even without a huge studio or complicated audio recording software, a decent mike that connects via USB can get the job done. Most computers now will recognize an external mike, and if you really need to, you can always rerecord audio into the camera (it helps to have an audio input jack and a headphone jack included). Whether you need a voice over, creaking floor sounds, or punching noises for that fistfight, a single mike can get you there and bring your video to a higher level.

Once you have your mike, get ready to experiment. The other big secret about sound in films is that a huge portion of what you hear is not generated naturally. Picture a dark detective flick. The lead character slowly makes his way down an alley, following a suspect. Each movement brings a scrape of hard-soled shoes on the concrete, as the suspense builds. Sounds great, right? I don't know about you, but my shoes never make so much noise. If you could listen to the raw production sound, you would notice that shoes actually make very little sound. Foley artists match each on-screen movement with a pair of shoes "worn" on their hands, shifting and sliding and scraping them against a patch of concrete near a good mike (Figure 91.1). It's fascinating to watch and incredibly effective. I once saw two foley specialists record six tracks of audio for a scene of a Civil War army marching through a town. On the first pass, the shots were not that effective. After the foley artists worked their magic, shaking belts and swords and tin coffee mugs, the scene ran again and the ground shook! The army came to life, the town folks seemed truly afraid, and the shots turned into a *scene*.

So, whether you need just a touch of audio or layers of sound, be prepared to take a close look at the footage — with your ears! Make an honest list of what might help the scene come to life, plug in your mike, and start tracking, creaking, scraping, and clinking.

Figure 91.1

92
TALKING THE TALK

A few years back, a buddy of mine made a short movie on an old film camera, one that could not record any audio at all. The film was great, but what really floored me was that he recorded all the audio (dialogue, foley, music, sound effects) after the final edit was done. Here's how you can do the same thing.

Let's say that you shoot a short video about a person getting up, making coffee, getting dressed, and leaving through the front door. And let's say that this person is concerned about the day ahead, full of thoughts and worries. The only problem? You can't shoot thoughts or worries. So we know you'll need some narration. Now let's assume that you actually shoot this epic, and that it runs less than three minutes. Go ahead; I'll wait while you shoot and complete a quick edit. . . .

Done? Next you need to watch the piece with an ear for what audio you need to record in post. Your list might begin with the most obvious elements: narration, music, and foley. I'll leave the creation of the narrative and the music up to you. As for the foley, here's my list of what is missing: alarm clock, sheets, soft steps (no shoes), water running, coffee pot noises, radio in background, clothes (including zippers, belt, shoes, and whatever else is shown), pouring coffee, mug clinks, coffee sips, props (keys, bag, umbrella, whatever is used by the actor), door opening and closing.

Did I get everything? Feel free to add anything I missed. Now, before you start recording, grab an empty box (like the kind that holds reams of copy paper) and either some foam or thin carpet. Cut the foam or the carpet to line the inside of the ream box, and stuff it into place (use tape or glue if needed). Carefully carve a small hole through the back of the ream box and the foam, dead center. Run your mike cable through this hole and place your mike (and small mike stand) inside this mini-studio (Figure 92.1). The foam and box will help to isolate the sounds recorded by the mike and block out any unwanted background noises from neighbors, curious roommates, or air conditioners.

Plan to record all of one type of audio at a time. Group the sounds from your list into categories (clothing, kitchen sounds, background, narrations) and record them group by group. Record more clinks and clangs than you think you need. You may want to try different combinations matched against the edit to achieve the most believable effect. If possible, you should watch the scene as you record the audio, and some programs will even let you do both at once. The idea is to build a small library of sounds, import them into the editing software, and mix and match as needed.

A last note: There are a ton of sound effects online. That's the good news. Most of them are available for free or are inexpensive, as long as you include the proper recognition in your credits. The bad news is that you may need a particular sound or a longer, louder, or bolder sound. And you don't want your piece to be full of audio that loads of other videos are also using. As for music, I would try to avoid using copyrighted material whenever possible, unless you specifically have permission from the artist or rights holder. Consider asking a local band or local musicians to use one of their songs: They could use the support, and they might just hire you to direct their next video!

Figure 92.1

TIP 93
EMBRACING THE SONIC ONION

My apartment is located across from a significant intersection near New Haven, Connecticut, above a set of sidewalks and close to the main entrance for the building. My door shares a common hallway and the whole shebang sits above two other apartments. What's the point of this random revelation? On any given day, my experience is defined by the layers of sound that merge together, audio both from my apartment (music, phone, refrigerator hum) and from nearby (traffic, voices, doors creaking and slamming shut). You need to start envisioning your videos in the same way: as worlds that are defined by layers of audio.

First, let's sort out a few important distinctions. The score and the soundtrack of a film are related, but distinctly different. A score consists of music created specifically for a film, which often is played and recorded to correspond to the final edit, matching or supporting key dramatic moments. The soundtrack is the collection of songs that most likely exist in and of themselves, but may appear either *in the action* of the film (a character turns on a radio), or *in support of* the on-screen action (a rock song used to highlight a montage). The soundtrack, of course, is also the physical portion of the media (tape, film) that contains the audio information (whether analog or digital).

Dialogue consists of words that are spoken on screen by the characters, while narration is an additional source of spoken material, usually presented in voice over (see Tip 99). Foley, as you know, is the process of recording sounds that are caused by actors (walking, using props), while special-effect sounds are more specific to the production (explosions, laser blasts, vehicles sounds, and so forth). Atmospheric sounds complete the picture: They might include everything from low traffic sounds, to waves, to a dog barking in the distance. This often overlooked layer of audio can make the difference between a low-rent video and a memorable piece of cinema: It's all about completing the atmosphere in a way that is both organic to the moments in the film and believable (if nearly imperceptible) to your audience.

In any case, especially if you are working with dramatic material (fictional films, whether comedy or drama), be prepared to smother your final edit with layers of audio. Remember, most of what audiences experience is actually what they hear, more than what they see. It's not uncommon to see numerous tracks of audio supporting the final edit of a film. So go get those sound effects off the Web, record some crazy foley audio, work with a local musician to develop a score, and don't forget those subtle touches, like horns in traffic, clinking silverware, the low hum of a space heater, or the squawk of a walkie-talkie. In short, get ready to embrace the sonic onion.

TIP 94

THE EARS HAVE IT

A multitude of the sounds that you will eventually want to include in your videos will not actually be recorded during shooting. These include sounds like gunshots (because you're using toy guns, RIGHT?), punches, car crash sounds — basically anything violent, dangerous, or fun. But don't lose heart: All of these and more can be recreated using a decent mike and a little imagination without leaving your house. For all of these, keep in mind that the key is not to recreate the on-screen events or sources of the sounds, but to find safe, effective, and creative *alternatives* that fool your audience. Here are some fabulous tricks and imaginative solutions that you can capture for your videos.

For fight scenes and action shots, you may need to simulate punches, stabbing sounds, weapons, even the sound of snapping bones. For gunshots, start by popping a few balloons or paper lunch bags filled with air. For punches, try recording the sound of your own hands slapping together or your palm smacking against your thigh. For a beefier sound (pun intended), make a trip to the local deli counter. Top audio tricksters have spent years punching slabs of beef, raw chicken, and other commodities. The secret is getting the mike close enough to pick up the audio. You may want to wrap the mike in a sandwich bag to protect it. And be sure to wash your hands after you are done.

Another time-tested audio trick, used for ages in Hollywood, is to attack a piece of fruit with a pencil or a plastic knife (Figure 94.1). This is a great way to fake stabbing sounds. You can also experiment with smashing, bashing, or otherwise mutilating various kinds of apples, melons, and kiwis for all kinds of medically relevant sound effects. Snapping celery or other vegetables is a time-tested substitute for breaking bones or other gnarly injuries, including head wounds, falls, and crushing injuries. Ah, the joys of moviemaking! Bonus: This can also be a cheap way to feed your crew (kidding!).

For broken bones, a decent piece of balsa wood snapped near a mike can also do wonders. You can find these at hardware and hobby stores. Snapping wood also works for scenes in which an actor breaks through a door or crashes into a table. Too often, in real life, those dramatic moments actually don't sound that intense. Always be ready to fill out the sonic atmosphere in your video with a few key cracks of wood splintering, veggie snapping, or silverware toppling onto the ground.

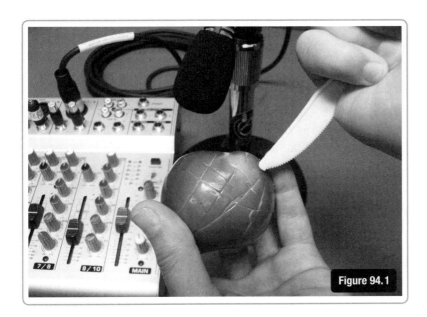

Figure 94.1

more dramatic smashes, you can build another type of crash box. This one is a three-sided wooden box that you place outside, in a safe area (like a backyard or a garage). With a mike near the box, you can throw bottles, metal, cans, or other objects into the crash box, which helps to control unwanted debris and pieces from flying around. I recommend safety goggles and work gloves; make sure that kids or random, unsuspecting folks are not around.

Lastly, here are a few cool environmental effects that you can capture. Rainstorms can happen in your sink or shower, thunder strikes can come from a metal panel or baking sheet, and a few marbles or metal bearings shimming across that same baking sheet can do wonders when simulating bigger storms or hail. A few carefully selected pieces of paper crumbled near the mike can simulate the sound of a burning campfire. While you are in the kitchen, consider using butter knives for sword sounds, a blender for an airplane or large machinery, and boiling water to complement shots of a mad scientist's laboratory. Oh, and be sure to feed your crew. Unless all you have is some raw chicken that you just punched for forty-five minutes. Good luck, have fun, and be safe.

For breaking glass, borrow an old theater trick. Build a box out of thin wood and some wire mesh, including a lockable flap on one side. Wrap a few bottles in an old towel or worksheet and *carefully* break them with a hammer. Drop the broken pieces into the box, and shake or roll the box near your mike. This will cause a heck of a lot of noise, but the shards stay in the box and not on your floor. For

TIP 95
WHEN SOUND COMES FIRST

Playback is the act of running pre-recorded sound during the shoot and is most common for productions like music videos. At first glance, this may seem like the easiest challenge you will face, and in some respects this is true. Still, there are a few tips to consider before you hit "play" and roll tape. Here goes.

For music videos, it's crucial to sync up any pre-recorded audio with the visual performance, especially if you are filming while the band plays along. First, take the time to bring a PA (public-address) system or loud stereo to the shoot, as the drums and cymbals alone can interfere with hearing the playback. An MP3 player with two headsets may not be enough. Also, make sure to run an additional audio feed from the playback device to the camera. You won't use this in the final edit, but having an audio track synced in the camera to the performance will save you heaps of headaches during the edit. For instances when you are just shooting the singer on a street or in a cornfield, this won't

work. You may, in fact, need to get by with just a music player (if the singer needs earphones, hide the cable under a shirt or scarf). But you can still split the audio cables and run a feed into the camera for reference.

A similar execution involves movies in which a band plays in the shot: a rock band at a nightclub or a classical quartet at a dinner party. Treat this like a music video, even if it means fading out the playback during the shot. For example, picture a jazz band onstage in a club. As the band plays along and the shot pans to a corner booth where your characters deliver dialogue, dump the playback after the shot leaves the stage. And take the time to link the performances to the audio. Nothing drives me crazy faster than shots of drummers playing the hi-hat when the music contains a blazing ride cymbal part or a violinist slowly bowing when the music is actually up-tempo.

For some dramatic moments, you may need characters to react to a pre-recorded piece. For example, picture a gathering of army generals reacting to a desperate radio call from their soldiers. Or picture a CIA agent screening a crucial clip from a doomed informant. In each case, create the pre-recorded piece in its entirety before shooting the remainder of the scene. You may eventually use this audio in the final edit, but you'll need your actors to see and hear it on-set to capture good performances.

Last, there are reasons for playing audio that may not directly correlate to the images on-screen. For example, some directors play a particular piece of audio on-set simply to set the timing for a critical tracking shot. And some directors play music on-set to give their cast (and crew) a sense of the tone that they are trying to capture. These tracks may or may not appear in the final film, and it almost doesn't matter: Just remember that there are several ways to use audio to make the best video that you can.

#96 GET WILD!

So you've got all the shots, the scene was performed brilliantly, and now you can break for lunch, right? Not so fast. There are a number of crucial pieces of on-set audio that you need to think about capturing because they can make (or break) your video and also because you may never get a chance to grab them again.

The first on your list of production sounds to capture is called room tone. "Room" or just "tone" is crucial to save the sanity of editors near and far. It consists of capturing the actual sound of the room in which you shoot, whether you're in a studio or on location. Factors that influence the overall audio character of a room include electrical hum (yes, AC current has a subtle hum, the reason why power outages are always so quiet); refrigerator and other appliance motors; air conditioners; fans; nearby traffic (vehicular and human); and the size, shape and composition of the space itself (wood rooms sound different than concrete rooms). This is also dictated by the number of people in the room, so you should grab room tone with your cast and crew present.

You only need about thirty seconds of "clean" room tone (no talking, no keys jingling, no phones), and it can be tough getting a crew of seventeen people to settle in for that long. But this small piece of audio proves *crucial* for "patching" edits, almost like audio spackle. You may have a shot that works visually, but you need to dump the sound, or you may have two shots next to one another, but a crew member sneezes in one and you need to fix that spot. In either case, dropping a spot of room tone under the video can keep the overall picture seamless,

providing a "bed" of natural sound and ensuring a smooth stream of audio free from strange gaps or hiccups.

The second batch of clips that you need to record after shooting are called "wild tracks." They are "wild" because they originate from the scene, but are recorded free of their visual counterpart. For example, horror movies are always packed full of screams and shrieks. But often, during the shooting of a scene, the scream may distort or be recorded poorly. Sometimes the audio isn't captured at all. In any case, your audio engineer should let you know so that you can grab the performer to record a few bonus screams without worrying about reshooting the images. This can be done quickly with a mike and a deck or a mike and the camera. Almost any piece of dialogue can become wild, either for a technical reason or to ensure a proper vocal performance. The director and audio crew should decide together what is needed, but get it while you are on-set. This is always better than tracking down the actor later and trying to match the audio quality to the conditions found during the shoot.

Similarly, you may want to grab additional audio effects or performances on location. These include noises made by certain props (squeaking doors, creaking floors), particular vehicles, or the sounds of the location itself (a ballpark, a car wash). If time allows, you might take a few minutes to grab similar audio for use in other projects or to build your library of audio effects. Also, certain locations, like the stairwells in a parking garage, may provide a cool reverb effect, and you can record some cool audio once the main scenes are shot.

Lastly, never hesitate to get as much out of your actors as you can. You might want to record a speech that appears later in the film, a second take of a particularly challenging vocal performance, or just a few words promoting the film that you can throw into a podcast later. I worked on a film once that included a character who may or may not have been insane. I worked with the director, audio crew, and actress to schedule an hour for her just to read lines into the mike. During this session, she was able to give us numerous takes, each one more bizarre than the next, which allowed the director a great deal of flexibility for fine-tuning her performance during the editing of the film.

97
YE OLDE FISHING POLE

It's an image as iconic as the camera itself: a mike on a boom swinging into position in order to capture the slightest breath of dialogue. The boom, also known as the "fishing pole," has served film crews for ages, and if your project calls for it, it can help you out as well.

First of all, be aware that most booms work with mikes that require an XLR cable, so be sure your camera has an XLR input, or use an external deck or adaptor. Second, the biggest issue that faces most unseasoned boom operators is the cable itself. Make sure that you secure the cable with Velcro straps or rubber bands (no tape!), so that it doesn't flap against the pole. This seemingly innocent clang can cause havoc with your audio.

Third, good booming is all about position. The skull is a strange thing: It actually reverberates sound in all directions, not just from the mouth. So dropping a boom about a foot above your actors, perpendicular to the floor, is optimal (Figure 97.1). Remember that this may require a "frame check," to make sure that the mike isn't dipping into the shot or that the pole isn't casting any shadows. Once this is set, you should be good to roll tape, and you'll end up with solid audio.

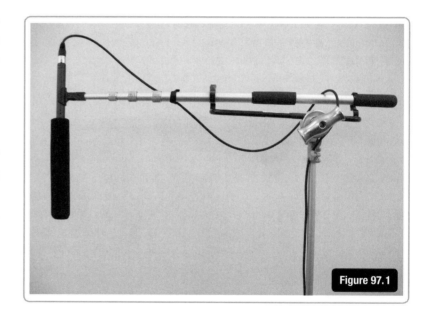

Figure 97.1

In the case of two actors who are fairly spread apart, you may want to rotate the boom slightly for each line of dialogue, pointing the mike at a slight angle to face each actor, but still primarily capturing the audio from above. In the case of an extremely wide shot, where the boom just won't reach, do the best you can, but be sure to track the same lines as wild tracks after the shot is in the can.

For wild tracks, you can simply hold the boom at head height, like a traditional mike stand, to grab the audio. Be sure to adjust your input levels so that there is no distortion. And please be careful: Actors tend to be fairly sensitive types who would rather not get bonked on the head with an errant boom. Mind the lights and such as well, and try not to damage the location. For a busy set or a situation with a lot of cables, consider keeping one crew member assigned to handle the XLR cable trailing after the boom, keeping it free from obstacles and feet. Your boom operator should focus on the position of the mike, and the extra help and increased safety will prove valuable.

TIP 98
POP GOES THE SAILOR

Your shoot is over, the final edit is locked, and yet… something is still missing. After a careful viewing of the project, you realize that you still need something, but you can't quite see what it is: Remember that what's missing might not be what you see at all. Here are a few more tips about audio and recording quality sound.

When tracking audio, use your surroundings to the best of your ability. Bathrooms, staircases, and hallways (if you have a long audio cable) can provide natural reverb effects for your audio, and offer a variety of sonic "colors." You may also benefit from adding more foam (to deaden sound) or placing a plank of wood near the mike (to brighten the audio or deflect more sound waves into the mike).

Mike selection, of course, is crucial to getting good audio (Figure 98.1). For most applications, the Shure SM58 covers all the bases. A decent shotgun mike is more expensive, but can capture accurate audio from a distance. Both require an XLR cable, so you may need an adaptor unless you are using an external mixer. USB driven mikes have improved in quality, capture a wide variety of audio, and are becoming more affordable. Crown makes an all-purpose condenser mike called a PZM that is affordable, easy to use (it comes with a simple 1/8" phono cable), and cleanly captures audio from voices to effects.

Figure 98.1

For location shoots, especially indoor shoots such as interviews, conferences, or focus groups, the PZM is an excellent solution. You can also use it for capturing dialogue in traditional scenes. Make some practice recordings before the real shoot, so that you are familiar with what audio levels work best with the mike(s) you plan to use. If you are booming, especially in an outdoor environment, invest in a good windscreen for the mike. These are the furry devices that you see on the end of boom poles, and they serve to lessen wind noise and higher frequencies that degrade your overall audio. On a tight budget? Use a piece of foam or a fluffy winter cap (Figure 98.2).

but these pops can ruin an otherwise clean recording. If you want to make your own, simply attach some old pantyhose to a wire hanger, bent into a rough circle and taped to the mike stand. Or use those wooden craft circles from a fabric shop.

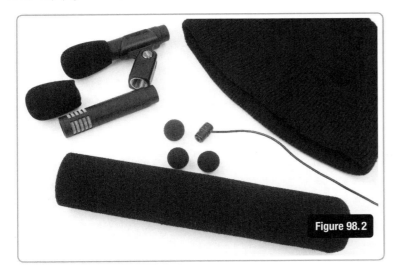

Figure 98.2

For those moments when you need to rerecord at home or in the studio, be sure to keep the mike away from unwanted sources of audio. These include refrigerators, AC units, and heaters. Fridges can also cause havoc on location. Many professional sound guys actually turn off the fridge on location and leave their car keys inside it. This ensures that they will remember to turn the fridge back on at the end of the shoot (it gets ugly if they forget — trust me). Another cheap investment, especially if you are aiming to record lots of voice over or dialogue in post, is a simple device called a pop guard (Figure 98.3). This is a thin filter, usually housed in a plastic circle, that clamps on to the mike stand and prevents sounds like "Ps" and "Ts" from causing unwanted pops and spikes in the recording. This may not seem like much,

Figure 98.3

TIP 99
RASPBERRIES AND ELEPHANT SHOES

There are numerous reasons to rerecord vocal performances during postproduction. After problems with the production sound, the most common reason is that you want to record either a voice over or narration. In either of these cases, the first thing you need to decide is whether or not the audio needs to follow the on-screen events specifically. If so, you'll need to complete and lock your edit before you add voice.

Just to clarify, voice over in news usually works against B-roll, so you will want to match the audio performance against a final picture. In dramatic applications (films, comedies), a voice over is generated by a character who participates in the drama. A narration, by contrast, is generated by a performer who may not be an active element in the story (a famous actor narrating an environmental documentary about, say, penguins). If you are adding voice to animation, the reverse is true: The vocal performance is always captured first, and then the picture is created to match.

There are also several types of vocal performances that you may need to capture. "Background" tracks refer to additional audio recorded to complete the sonic environment (customers in a diner or crowd noise at a hockey rink are two examples). The film term *ADR* either stands for *automatic dialogue replacement* or *additional dialogue recording*, depending on whom you ask. In either case, ADR is an additional postproduction recording session for voices, such as background performers. One trick is to have your actors say nonsense words like *raspberries* or *elephant shoes*, which serve as a way to generate content without specific words that may interfere with the main dialogue. Again, this works best for shots like crowd scenes. Of course, you could always have your actors carry on a normal conversation or read the newspaper, for that matter, but it's sometimes better to stick to nonsense vocals to prevent any embarrassing content from slipping into your movie.

More dramatic performances, of course, may be needed, especially for action scenes and war movies. You can always write lines ahead of time, but pay attention to the overall pace and tone of the scene. You don't want to end up with ADR tracks that pull attention away from the primary action. Some professional background performers work best in groups, with each member of a team picking particular elements to recreate. An example might be a crowded train station, where various elements (passengers, conductors, vendors) need to be addressed. If it's just you, try a few tricks to disguise your voice in the various tracks. For a PA system announcer, you can try talking through a tin can or plastic cup. For deeper sounds, talk with your mouth next to an empty coffee can. Explore recording with the mike at various distances from your mouth. One last tip: Don't worry about getting really loud tracks. This is background noise and should be fairly quiet. Try lowering the overall audio level during postproduction.

TIP 100
WHEN IS A STICK NOT A STICK

All this fancy audio talk is great, but what happens if you are on an extremely tight budget and can't afford a proper boom pole (Figure 100.1)? Well, just look for a stick.

In a pinch, a homemade boom pole is almost always a better option than relying on in-camera audio. You can fashion one from a broom, a hockey stick, or almost any form of dowel. But beware: Avoid the classic mistake of taping the mike and cable in place. Tape is always a nightmare to remove, and it leaves a nasty, sticky residue on cables. To secure the cable, try rubber bands or those plastic clips that are used to close bags of chips. As for the mike, this can be a bit trickier. The key is obviously not to let the mike slip off the pole. If you have a mike clip, this can help a lot, as you only need to secure it with a rubber band. If not, you may need to create a clip. You can do this using cardboard or by building a wire holder out of a coat hanger, solder, or picture-hanging wire.

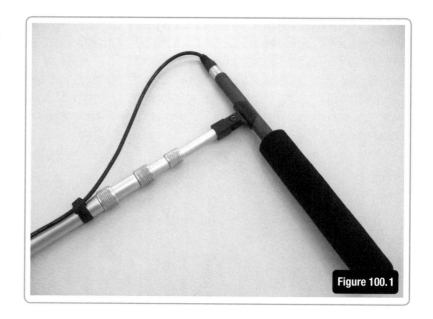

Figure 100.1

Another clever solution is to use a traditional stage mike stand and simply unscrew the stand from the heavy metal base at the bottom. Now you can swing this pole into position, just like a proper boom, using a clip to secure the mike. Great, but what about those times when you have no such resources nearby, or if the broom you were using breaks halfway through the shoot?

Hiding mikes in the shot itself is normally not the best idea, but in this extreme case, it may just save you. You can pop a mike behind a plant or sometimes *in* the plant (depending on the shot). Depending on the *scene*, you may be able to get your actor to hold a mike behind a prop such as a file folder, briefcase, or a large cup. You can sneak mikes behind phones, computer monitors, or a pile of clothes. You may even be able to get away with keeping the mike in actors' laps, especially if they can deliver their lines with a little more punch than normal.

Finally, in some instances, you may be able to hang a mike off a piece of the architecture or a low-slung tree branch. Again, in such circumstances, be sure to secure the mike and cable carefully, so nothing slips out of place and crashes down on your cast during a scene or a rehearsal. Also, try to avoid using lighting stands or tripods to hold mikes: This tends to get messy and will not endear you to the lighting, grip, or camera crews.

Finally, I should note that wireless mike kits are becoming more and more affordable, and it may be worth saving up a little and investing in a set (Figure 100.2).

These wireless sets consist of a small unit that is worn on the belt or in the pocket of your actor. This is the unit that transmits the signal. A similar unit acts as a receiver, and some come with a tab that can slide into the shoe (the small metal slot on top of most camcorders) and tighten into place. Be sure that your camera and wireless set come with matching audio cables/input jacks, and be sure to test the whole shebang before you shoot. You'll want to find out what the actual range is for transmitting the signal and how the overall audio comes out in the final recording.

Figure 100.2

TEN BY TEN, POP, FIZZ, WILD AND WOOLLY

HERE ARE SOME FUN EXERCISES FOR GETTING YOUR AUDIO UNDER CONTROL.

1. Start researching online sources for good audio files now; it will save you stress and drama later (especially if your video is up against a deadline).

2. Play with mikes. Visit a local audio store and check out as many as you can. Know them backwards and forwards. Which ones sound better? Deeper? Thinner? Cleaner? What audio adapters do you need for your camera? For your computer?

3. Practice setting the audio levels. Does your camera allow for adjustments to the audio input levels? How does this change the sound of the in-camera mike? What about an external mike? How does the placement of the mike affect the levels?

4. Record a short paragraph in your kitchen (this could be from a newspaper, a script, or the Gettysburg Address). Next, rerecord the same words in your bathroom, a subway station, or a stairwell. How does the audio change?

5. Rewind! Pick your favorite mini-scene from the exercises in this book. Now delete all the audio from the source recordings (not on the tape, in your editing software!), and rerecord all the sounds for the scene.

6. Shoot a three-minute sequence of friends playing catch, street hockey, or video games. Digitize the footage and then record you or a friend doing play-by-play and color commentary. Be sure to dub in some cheering crowd noise!

7. Go shopping! Grab a selection of the finest fruits, vegetables, and raw meats. Then bash, poke, crack, smash, and stab the meat to your heart's content. It's best if you do this at home, by the way, preferably near a good microphone.

8. The shoes have it! Try recording some foley shoe sounds. Try to record as many different types of scrapes, clomps, and clicks as possible. Experiment with different shoes, speeds, slides, and surfaces. Remember, people walk in all kinds of ways, on all types of surfaces, in many, many types of footwear.

9. Try creating an entire summer thunderstorm using only self-generated sound effects (no downloads!). Bonus if you shoot rainstorm footage first, to match.

10. Remember that "restaurant" scene, in your kitchen? Make this video soar by adding ADR sounds of people, waiters, phones, clinking glasses, and scrapping silverware.

CONCLUSION

TIP 101
FINAL THOUGHTS

Clearly, you have some homework to do — lots of exercises, shots, and tricks to practice. With a little work, a sharp eye, and a dose of dedication, it will all come together (Figure 101.1), and your videos will begin to improve. I still can't guarantee that you'll get more views than videos featuring a snowboarding squirrel or a guy passing out at his own wedding, but I can promise that by using the tips and tricks in this book, *your* videos will look better, sound better, and leave your audiences wanting more.

Do not get frustrated if some of these techniques don't work at first or if you struggle to execute them as smoothly or as effectively as you imagine: With a bit of practice and a willingness to learn from your mistakes, your work will grow and improve. Run through the more complex tips before you go on-set. Force yourself to practice even the simplest shots (pans, tilts) until you can knock them off in your sleep. And watch as many videos as you can: There are a ton of poor videos out there with fuzzy graphics, terrible lighting, and garbled audio. Even top-notch pros sometimes miss a shot, load an incorrect graphic, or run the same three B-roll shots over and over in a story. Learning from the

mistakes of others (pros and beginners), as well as from their successes, will inform your own work, pushing you to produce better and better video as time goes along. Try to recreate the great shots you see in your favorite films or the amazing lighting you saw in a music video. See if you can build graphics and transitions and audio tracks that work as well as the professional examples we see all the time.

And push yourself to post. There may be lots of footage that you never want the world to see (practice pans that shake and shimmy, for example). But if you pull off a great green-screen shot using a sheet and a desk lamp, tell the world how you made it happen. Shoot behind-the-scenes footage, interviews with other filmmakers, and document your greatest failures. Above all, keep those batteries charged, a tripod in the trunk, and your camera ready to roll. I look forward to seeing your work!

Figure 101.1

TEN BY TEN, FINAL THOUGHTS

HERE ARE SOME FINAL WORDS OF ADVICE AS YOU HEAD OUT TO CONQUER YOUTUBE.

1. Get permission. Just because your uncle works at the local train yard doesn't mean you can wander all over the tracks to get that perfect shot.

2. Put it in writing. There are numerous resources where you can find location agreements, deal memos (for crew members), contracts, and image releases. The last thing you want is for your video to go viral, only to get sued by the coffee shop where you shot for not obtaining their official blessing.

3. Keep your lens clean, your tripod in good shape, and your computer free of junk. Your gear is crucial; treat it well, and it will treat you well.

4. Buy an external hard drive on which to store media: video clips, audio tracks, graphics. Keeping everything on the main drive will slow performance and gunk up the works. Be sure to back up your work often: Hard drive crashes don't come with an "undo" option.

5. Feed your crew. Nothing inspires a crew to work harder, and with a better attitude, than a decent meal and a chance to relax and recharge. Bring extra napkins.

6. Shoot first; ask questions later. There's a huge advantage to planning each shot, each location, each edit in great detail. But sometimes you can't get everything ironed out in advance. There's an old film belief that shooting helps to work out the kinks, and this is often true. When in doubt, shoot first and work out any problems as they come along.

7. Don't break any property, laws, or promises. Everything else can be mended.

8. Shoot more than you think you need. Time is money, but tape is cheap.

9. Don't believe everything that a potential producer, investor, actor, or editor tells you (especially online). Ask for a resume, headshot, reel, or reference. You don't want anyone on your crew with whom you wouldn't want to have a cup of coffee.

10. Don't stop dreaming, or learning, or asking questions. And remember that old Hollywood maxim: You're only as good as your last film. So get out there and keep shooting (especially if you can get an epic tracking shot of that snowboarding squirrel).

END
APPENDIX ▶

Uploading

Okay, here's one last video secret that I'll share: I'm terrible at uploading videos. Not horrible, but let's just say it isn't my favorite way to spend an afternoon. The first experience I had while uploading a clip to YouTube, for example, way back in the dark ages of 2007, was a complete nightmare. I would click upload, walk away, and two hours later the status bar was still creeping along. Thankfully, uploading has become easier and sites like YouTube have done wonders with improving the look and sound of online videos, as well as increasing the length of each video that you can post.

For starters, numerous online help options exist; you can check a number of Web-based forums, and the YouTube Creator's Corner is also a fantastic aid. No matter your approach, to master uploading and minimize headaches, you'll need to become familiar with codecs, programs that compress and decompress video files (codec simply being a lingual shortcut for **co**mpressor-**dec**ompressor). The bad news is that there are literally hundreds of such programs, with a dizzying number of possible combinations and options for video, audio, and other settings. The good news is that most editing programs have been updated to help take the pain of codecs away. Most feature export options that allow you to create files that are primed for YouTube specifically, taking the guesswork out of your upload.

For more advanced circumstances (musicians who are eager to maintain a certain fidelity in their audio, for example), I suggest making a trial video, playing with the various settings and codecs, writing down the choices you made, and then uploading the file. Does it play correctly? Is it grainy or pixilated? Does the audio sound "squished"? If so, delete that file from the site and try another combination or codec. If your file is simply too large, you may also need to get familiar with programs that specifically work to compress your files. And again, the good news is that while these retain a high level of flexibility (allowing you to customize settings), most current compression software features pre-set options for YouTube and other options (cell phones, for example). The long, dark uploading nightmare is ending.

Best bet? Grab some footage or completed edits that you have made during the course of exploring this book, cram the final file through a codec, and pop it online. Check the playback. Call friends and get their opinion. Watch it on your phone *and* on your computer. If it works, *write down the settings* and keep uploading. If there is an issue with the quality, delete it, reconfigure your codes, and try again. That just might be the best part of all this: If your upload fails, there are probably 4,743 people out there in Web-land who had the same issue and who posted their solutions. Just keeping plugging away and don't get frustrated. After all, I still find myself compressing and then recompressing completed videos to get the right settings, and I *literally* wrote the book on all this craziness! If I can manage to survive the madness of exporting and uploading, surely so can you.

FILM AND VIDEO REFERENCES

The author acknowledges the copyright owners of the following motion pictures, independently produced films, and independently produced videos from which single frames have been used in this book for purposes of commentary, criticism, and scholarship under the Fair Use Doctrine.

MOTION PICTURES

Big Fish, © 2003 Columbia Pictures Industries, Inc., all rights reserved.

Citizen Kane, © 1941, RKO Pictures, Inc., all rights reserved.

Dead Poets Society, © 1989 Buena Vista Pictures / Touchstone Pictures, all rights reserved.

Fear and Loathing in Las Vegas, © 1998 Universal City Studios, Inc., all rights reserved.

Once Upon a Time in the West, © 1968 Paramount Pictures Corporation, all rights reserved.

Punch-Drunk Love, © 2002 Revolution Studios Distribution Company, LLC, all rights reserved.

The Shawshank Redemption, © 1994 Castle Rock Entertainment, all rights reserved.

The Usual Suspects, © 1995 PolyGram Film Productions B.V., all rights reserved.

INDEPENDENT FILMS AND VIDEOS

Bottles, © 2007 Joe DeFillippo and Angel Tirado

Factory Girl, © 2007 Pyrom E and Derek Ravita

Jornada del Muerto, © 1999 Matthaeus Szumanski

Mix 'n Mingle, © 2008 the author

Pass the Puck, © 2008 the author

Time Out with the Zambonis, © 2008 the author

YJTV Ch. 19 *Student News*, © 2009 East Haven School District/YJTV Ch. 19

Words, © 2007 Brian Katsis

PHOTOGRAPHS

All photographs by the author unless otherwise noted. Models: Krista Aldrich and Tanya Andrasko. Author portrait by Desirea Rodgers. Additional photos by Krista Aldrich, Heather Berner, Melissa Morro, and Derek Ravita. Special thanks to Adam Meltzer and Turnkey HD (turnkeyhd.com) for the use of their production photos.

BIO Author

Jay Miles began his video journey during high school in the suburbs of Washington, D.C., when he was selected to join the cast of a cable access student-news show called *Student's Corner*.

Completing a bachelor's degree in technical theater at the University of Virginia, Jay worked on lights, sound, and set construction for countless plays, concerts, and live events. Jay next completed a master's degree in TV, Radio and Film at Syracuse University's S.I. Newhouse School of Public Communications. He contributed to marketing and promotions campaigns, events, and videos for numerous clients, bands, record labels, and PR firms. His major Los Angeles production credits include shows for NBC, ABC, FOX, Discovery, Britain's Channel 4, Warner Brothers, and numerous films, music videos, live concerts, industrials, and commercials.

Jay Miles

Beginning in 2001, Jay began teaching video, audio, and media, enjoying positions with Syracuse University, Gibbs College, and the Connecticut School of Broadcasting. He currently teaches at East Haven High School (CT), where his students' videos have won several awards. Jay continues to work in the industry, most recently in the control room for *NHL on Versus*, *US Open* (tennis), and as a field producer for HGTV.

Jay looks forward to seeing your videos conquer YouTube, and can be reached via his site, *www.jmilestv.com*.

Jay Miles lives in New Haven, Connecticut.

MAKING IT BIG IN SHORTS
2ND EDITION
THE ULTIMATE FILMMAKER'S GUIDE TO SHORT FILMS

KIM ADELMAN

Grab a camera, make a short film. Show it at Sundance; show it on YouTube. There's no limit to what you can achieve by starting small and dreaming big.

In easy-to-follow steps, short-film guru, Kim Adelman, shows you how to achieve your dreams by making that killer short film. Bringing together the artistic and business sides of filmmaking, this book gives filmmakers the skills to develop unique shorts that are creatively satisfying and can launch careers.

This Second Edition of the best-selling *The Ultimate Filmmaker's Guide to Short Films* addresses new avenues for short filmmakers, including 48-hour filmmaking challenges, and new media opportunities such as YouTube, iTunes, and the iPhone.

If you want to make it big in short films, this is the book you need.

"Kim is the undisputed queen of the short-film world. No one has a better resume, better relationships, and more passion for this particular art form than she does, and her willingness to share this knowledge, especially the hard-won lessons, is inspiring."
> — Mark Stolaroff, producer/founder,
> No Budget Film School

"An essential guide for anybody who wants to make short films, which is great, because I love the short-film format. It's the best!"
> — Bill Plympton, Oscar-nominated
> animator: *Guard Dog, I Married a Strange Person, www.plymptoons.com*

"A practical, down-to-earth, soup-to-nuts manual on getting the most out of the short-film experience — from succinct tips on all phases of production, to making the most out of the film festival experience, and beyond. A must-read for any filmmaker who values thorough advice delivered with energy, humor, and a sincere affection for the medium."
> — Christian Gaines, director of festivals,
> Withoutabox – a division of IMDb.com

KIM ADELMAN produced 19 short films that played at over 150 film festivals, worldwide, and won 30+ awards. She currently is the short-film correspondent for the acclaimed independent film news service indieWIRE. Additionally, Adelman teaches "Making and Marketing the Short Film" and "Low Budget Filmmaking" at UCLA Extension, and leads filmmaking workshops across the United States, Canada, and New Zealand.

$22.95 | 264 PAGES | ORDER NUMBER 128RLS | ISBN: 9781932907582

MASTER SHOTS
100 ADVANCED CAMERA TECHNIQUES TO GET AN EXPENSIVE LOOK ON YOUR LOW-BUDGET MOVIE

CHRISTOPHER KENWORTHY

Master Shots gives filmmakers the techniques they need to execute complex, original shots on any budget. By using powerful master shots and well-executed moves, directors can develop a strong style and stand out from the crowd. Most low-budget movies look low-budget, because the director is forced to compromise at the last minute. *Master Shots* gives you so many powerful techniques that you'll be able to respond, even under pressure, and create knock-out shots. Even when the clock is ticking and the light is fading, the techniques in this book can rescue your film, and make every shot look like it cost a fortune.

Each technique is illustrated with samples from great feature films and computer-generated diagrams for absolute clarity.

Use the secrets of the master directors to give your film the look and feel of a multi-million-dollar movie. The set-ups, moves and methods of the greats are there for the taking, whatever your budget.

"Master Shots *gives every filmmaker out there the blow-by-blow setup required to pull off even the most difficult of setups found from indies to the big Hollywood blockbusters. It's like getting all of the magician's tricks in one book.*"
— Devin Watson, producer, *The Cursed*

"*Though one needs to choose any addition to a film book library carefully, what with the current plethora of volumes on cinema,* Master Shots *is an essential addition to any worthwhile collection.*"
— Scott Essman, publisher,
Directed By Magazine

"*Christopher Kenworthy's book gives you a basic, no holds barred, no shot forgotten look at how films are made from the camera point of view. For anyone with a desire to understand how film is constructed — this book is for you.*"
— Matthew Terry, screenwriter/director,
columnist
www.hollywoodlitsales.com

Since 2000, CHRISTOPHER KENWORTHY has written, produced, and directed drama and comedy programs, along with many hours of commercial video, tv pilots, music videos, experimental projects, and short films. He's also produced and directed over 300 visual FX shots. In 2006 he directed the web-based Australian UFO Wave, which attracted many millions of viewers. Upcoming films for Kenworthy include *The Sickness* (2009) and *Glimpse* (2011).

$24.95 | 240 PAGES | ORDER NUMBER 91RLS | ISBN: 9781932907513

THE MYTH OF MWP

In a dark time, a light bringer came along, leading the curious and the frustrated to clarity and empowerment. It took the well-guarded secrets out of the hands of the few and made them available to all. It spread a spirit of openness and creative freedom, and built a storehouse of knowledge dedicated to the betterment of the arts.

The essence of the Michael Wiese Productions (MWP) is empowering people who have the burning desire to express themselves creatively. We help them realize their dreams by putting the tools in their hands. We demystify the sometimes secretive worlds of screenwriting, directing, acting, producing, film financing, and other media crafts.

By doing so, we hope to bring forth a realization of 'conscious media' which we define as being positively charged, emphasizing hope and affirming positive values like trust, cooperation, self-empowerment, freedom, and love. Grounded in the deep roots of myth, it aims to be healing both for those who make the art and those who encounter it. It hopes to be transformative for people, opening doors to new possibilities and pulling back veils to reveal hidden worlds.

MWP has built a storehouse of knowledge unequaled in the world, for no other publisher has so many titles on the media arts. Please visit www.mwp.com where you will find many free resources and a 25% discount on our books. Sign up and become part of the wider creative community!

Onward and upward,

Michael Wiese
Publisher/Filmmaker